MAN
WITHOUT
BORDERS

A BIOGRAPHY

of

DETERMINATION,

ENDURANCE

AND LOVE

Chris

a lecto con mente
con todo mi appo
su amigo

Bernardo Vago

Man Without Borders
Rosa Valdez-Robinson

This book is dedicated
to my parents,
Fernando Peréa Valdez and
Micaela Valenzuela Valdez,
with all my love for giving
unconditional love and time,
moral teachings and commitment
to ten children,
whom I believe
tried our best
to be our best.

The strength of the human spirit is brought to light when a man of 30 finally grasps the one and only opportunity to turn his life around.

His plight is worth learning from, and perhaps even worth taking a little gold nugget from, as he did from his father and his father's love during the Great Depression.

A quote Fernando lives by:

"Between individuals, as among nations, respect of the rights of others is peace."
Attributed: Benito Juarez, Mexican President 1867

"Entre los individuos, como entre las naciones, el respeto al derecho ajeno es la paz."
Attribuido: Benito Juarez, Mexican President 1867

4

Disclaimer

This is the true story of my father, Fernando, which was narrated and written over time. While some of the statistical facts are provided according to his memories and his father's life and information, various articles in books, periodicals or internet, dating back to the early 1900's can confirm much of it. Provided below are sources used.

Scholars may disagree on certain data, but the substance of the information produced here is mostly consistent with each other's research.

Sources used:

- Balderrama, Francisco E. (Professor and Dean, Natural and Social Sciences, CSU) and Rodriguez, Raymond (Emeritus); 1996 *Decade of Betrayal, Mexican Repatriation in the 1930s*, (2nd ed. 2006) Albuquerque, NM, University of New Mexico Press.

- https://www.history.com/
  "The U.S. Deported One Million of Its Own to Mexico During the Great Depression." Becky Little, July 12, 2019

- https://www.npr.org/2015/09/10/43911456 3/americas-forgotten-history-of-mexican-american-repatriation

- *https://www.dualcitizenship.com/countries /mexico.html*

CHAPTER 1
A Familiar Place - 2018

CHAPTER 2
"Invitation" out of America -1930

CHAPTER 3
Migrant Field Raids -1930

CHAPTER 4
Deportation to Mexico - 1930

CHAPTER 5
Deeper South - 1933

CHAPTER 6
Lessons on Love and Death - 1935

CHAPTER 7
Transportation - 1935-1938

CHAPTER 8
Meeting Her, Losing Her - 1939

CHAPTER 9
Life Changes During World War II –
1940-1941

CHAPTER 10
Love, Marriage and Miscarriage -1943

CHAPTER 11
Pernicious Stranger - 1953

CHAPTER 12
Reclaiming My U.S. Birthright -1953

CHAPTER 13
Life is Sweeter on This Side - 2018

CHAPTER 14
My Freedom and U. S. Redemption
Tucson, AZ
2018

CHAPTER 1

A Familiar Place
2018

So much has changed. The landscape is different, with large homes, fancy restaurants and golf courses overtaking the small township it once was. I don't see any shacks or rural roads.

We passed a sign on the street nearby:

Welcome: Gilbert, AZ
Population 2018: 200,000

Population 1930: 500

We pull up to the Gilbert Heritage Museum in Arizona. The covered wagon and 1927 Model A Ford sitting in front of the building remind me of my childhood. My wife Micaela and I have been waiting for a good day to travel here, just 65 miles north of Tucson. She, my daughter and I walk up to some concrete arches on a porch-like area, then into a wide hallway in the museum. Just inside the door my body gets a strange chill. Some things have been transformed. I look around, and in seconds my brain has processed a lifetime.

The structure is distinct. I slightly remember the arches, but inside, the building looks big and empty, with a clean coat of white paint. It's evident that the two short vintage doors at the back of the large room are original. There is a sign on each door, with streaks of paint on the worn doors. One sign reads: "Boys," the other reads "Girls". I'm lacking clarity but somewhere in the back of my mind, I am certain I've been here before. Micaela takes my hand and tries to pull me forward to walk, but she is frail and restricted by my hesitation at the entry. She waits.

"Fernando, is this where you went to school?" she asks me hopefully, in Spanish, as she looks up at me from her small frame. "Is this it?"

I look at her for a moment and my heart feels warm again to see her expectant face. I nod. She has dementia, but today is a lucid day for her. Sometimes she forgets who people are, and other things, but she is looking at me with precise understanding. I am glad our daughter drove so we could talk and take in the view as a couple. She's made it her business to ensure I have peace once I affirm my existence, the identity I lost when I left this land so many years ago.

The moment feels like an eternity, but I finally take Micaela's elbow and prompt her forward. I don't want her to see my misty eyes or she'll experience my melancholy state. When you've been married 75 years you take on each other's emotions.

We walk as fast as we can, which is slow for our 96 and 94 years of age. We try to catch up to our daughter as she approaches the counter to talk to the clerk. She has brought us here because I need to settle life-long questions about this place.

At the desk, we speak with the guide, in both English and Spanish. It makes me happy that she speaks our language so Micaela can feel comfortable. She leads us down the bare hallway where the only sound is the echoed clack clacking of her high-heeled shoes on the tiled floor.

She enters a small old schoolroom on the right that's been preserved in its unique state. We walk in behind her into a classroom arranged exactly like the one I loved in first grade. There are several small desks straight ahead and a chalkboard about three feet from the floor.

I see books in a corner, and then my eyes rivet toward several large class photo albums with the "The Mexican School" title written across the top. This was where Hispanic looking, usually darker children who spoke Spanish, were separated from light-skinned American children to learn. So I went to the "Mexican School" because that's where I was directed to go, but I was light-skinned with green eyes, too. I guess it is because I spoke Spanish and someone was determined that that was where I should be.

My 12-year-old chubby bother Manuel walked to school by himself every day, but I don't think he showed up there. He used to come home way after school let out, smelling like smoke and with scruffy clothes like he might have had a fight. He was probably hanging out with kids who caused problems.

I approach to see the hand-made laminated albums, big as poster boards on display. There are only a few pages to each album, and two class pictures on a page. I take two of the albums to the child's desk and squeeze my body into it. I flip through a few pages of the class photos. Neither my brother's picture nor mine is there. He attended much more regularly than I, since I only went a few days to first grade.

Some of the names of the children in the pictures are written in on the lines beneath the photo. There are more empty lines than names. Those must be the ones whose identities were never attained. I recognize one boy who sat next to me in class and I talked with, but his name is not written in.

I can see that boy's face and hear his voice far away, as if in a dream.

"You don't know how to read yet", he says in Spanish on my first day, "so I will show you our "Boys" bathroom and you have to pay attention to that sign and use that one."

At recess someone shows me the "Mexican School" sign and I should memorize it. That's the door I am supposed to use to go into our building to learn.

I see the light-skinned blondish kids – "Americanos" or "gringos" as we call them -- walk in next door. No sign on that door. I wonder what they learn, and why I can't sit in that class. Once I walk into the wrong room by mistake and it is clean and cool in there. And the drinking fountain is right by the door. But I am sent to the Mexican School room.

I have green eyes and am light-skinned, too. Papá has blue eyes and light skin. He says he came from a family of Spaniards, far, far away in Spain; almost across the world from us. I don't know how far that is but he looks like he might be a gringo to me. I wonder if the teachers have ever seen Papá in

11

school because maybe I'm in the wrong classroom. If I only spoke English, I think to myself, I might be able to get in the other room. I am very curious.

As I look at a teacher on the front-page photo, I hear a soft call from another direction and it's her very recognizable soft voice, Ms. Lupe Vejar Varela. She asks me to step outside the room and into the hallway. I wonder what I did wrong.

"Fernando . . .Señor . . . you need to go to the cafeteria," is all she says. She hands me a meal ticket out of sight of other students. I've seen her give them to other kids, but today's my lucky day! I take the ticket, happy to go eat a full meal, and I know they get milk to drink.

I follow the smell of food, making it quicker for me to get there. I walk into the large room where it is served. Several kids are sitting at long tables, and one gets up quickly to show me how to go through the line. I stand behind another kid, where just in front of him, I see platters with eggs, tortillas, beans and potatoes. I've never seen that much food! A long piece of glass separates me from the buffet awaiting me. It looks like a meal for a king.

I know the lady behind the counter with a hairnet on; she is Señorita Gomez, who also helps kids during recess. I smile at her proudly. She smiles back. I can't believe everything I see laid out before me. I am anxious to eat! I feel happy. Wait till Papá hears about this!

I am so hungry, but I will try to eat slower because Papá has told me that it is bad manners to gulp down your food. In her clean white uniform now, Señorita Gomez serves my plate. She adds a small carton of milk. I smile at her again.

When we go out for recess, I see a couple of friends pointing at me. I don't know what they are saying, but I know they are talking about me. I wonder why, because we've been friends and now they laugh and run when they see me approach. I don't know what's going on. They come back to me and talk.

"Fernando, you don't even know that you are a poor kid! Only poor kids are sent to the cafeteria," one   of   them   says   to   me.
"Why does it matter if I'm poor or not? I'm hungry and I will eat when a meal is offered," I say it with no regret, happy that I ate.   I walk away from them not caring what they think.

But suddenly I feel ashamed of being mocked because I have done that to others who get free meals. We all know who they are. Now I realize I am one of them. This very day I become friends with the kids who get fed; and I continue to enjoy my meals. But it is a lesson I will remember it and I decide I will not make fun of anyone any more.

Yes, I was here; right in this building. It was 1930 and I was 7 years old.

For a moment, I forget where I am. And then I see my daughter, and my beautiful wife looking back up at me with her wrinkled soft smile. Our eyes connect. We both know this is what I sought. I am home.

CHAPTER 2

"Invitation" Out of America
1930

I walk home two miles by myself from the Mexican School that day, unusual for me because I seldom get to go. We have no transportation in our rural area. As I near our shack, I see two dark green uniforms with gringo faces standing on our threadbare porch. One has a big stomach. Their guns are holstered and their arms are crossed, talking to my Papá. He nods and smiles. My stomach rises to my throat and I hold my breath. The pounding of my heart stops me in place.

From where I am, I see Papá squint and the wrinkle between his eyes get deeper. Drops of sweat fall from his dark toasted face. His migrant work in the fields in the hot Arizona sun has done that to him. I ease up quietly near him and his eyes dart toward me.

"We are inviting you to leave Arizona," the big bellied-one tells Papá. "If you people don't have your permanent residence papers showing you can live in the United States, you will need to leave the country," he continues. He has a black patch with bright yellow lining on his sleeve, stretched by his big arm at the top. They are the U.S. Border Patrol. "You have one week to go back to Mexico or wherever you came from. . . . or you will be picked up at that time and you will go to jail. No questions asked."

I want to tell them Papá does not speak English. But neither do I. I can hear them talking as if far away, but why do they keep chattering if we don't understand?

Papá alternates his look from one officer to the other, staring straight into their eyes, nodding and showing his respect for authority. He is holding his worn, beige Stetson hat by the rim in one hand, with the other hand fisted up inside the bowl area. I have no idea if he knows what they're saying but I think he understands. One thing I know: this is not good.

"Yes, sir," Papá finally says. The only other phrase I've heard him say in English is "thank you."

Now he turns to us, my grandmother Mamá Angelita, two uncles and 7-year-old me, when we're all on the porch. My brother Manuel is still not home from school. He'll show up all ragged from some scuffle and make Papá worry about him once more. But maybe he could have helped us with his English if he was here.

"The Immigration Officers came to bring us an *invitation*," Papá says courteously in Spanish, eyes down toward me, the shortest of all. "*They are inviting us,*" he emphasizes, "to leave Arizona within a week, or they will pick us up then, and who knows where we will end up. We are a family and we will stay together. We will pack and we'll be leaving in three days after I get my check," he finishes.

As if wanting to be sure we understand, the two men in uniform just listen. They look around at the five of us now, including Papá, standing crowded on the porch. The boards might just crunch through to the bottom with the heavy guy. I hope he falls through the flimsy floor.

I feel the wrinkle between my own eyes getting deep. People say I look like Papá with my green eyes and light complexion. I don't know what it means that we have to leave, or where we'll go, but I see the adults stand in disbelief, eyes searching each other for answers.

The officers wait for questions, I guess, then they walk away without a word. The fat guy makes a note on his clipboard, tells his partner something and points to another house down the street. He touches his holster, and they both get in the Jeep. As they drive away the same one looks back laughing.

Papá looks up to see neighbors peering out from behind their paper-covered, tattered windows. Surely they are thanking God it's not them but they know their own days are limited.

My insides hurt at the look on Papá's face. His shoulders seem heavier now, and his abnormal six-foot frame has shrunken. He appears to be leaning over. For a minute everything is quiet.

"Let's all go inside and rest. We still have to leave in a week," Papá says, opening the door for us to walk in.

"But Manuel, you and the kids can stay here!" my 87-year-old grandmother, Mamá Angelita, rebels, whispering loudly in Spanish as soon as we walk in. "They won't do anything to the kids! They can't put them in jail. They need a parent with them! She anxiously reminds Papá that there is no work in Mexico. He just stares at her without answering.

Every night, she holds her homemade rosary in her small hands. She prays morning and evening that we can stay and make our living in the U.S. She knows where the family came from and the possibility of our surviving it in Mexico's poverty-stricken condition is not very good. Where will they work, she asks? What will they do? She has heard there are posters and newspaper articles around town to scare illegal immigrants into leaving or they will be deported, they say. But she prays anyway.

I guess I'm an illegal immigrant since I am part of the family, and I have to go, too. Maybe it will be a good trip, who knows. I will get to see another place. I am used to being home.

"Madre," Papá says firmly to my grandmother. "I am a legal resident of the U.S., but if the rest of you cannot stay here with me, then we all go. Our family stays together," he reassures her just as she had hoped to hear. She lets out a short quiet breath when he walks away.

"Mamá Angelita, I want to go wherever Papá goes or stays!" I say. I think she is like 100 years old and I don't want to hurt her feelings. She knows I love her, but I love Papá more.

I always hang around him and can't imagine living without him. Where would I go? I already don't have a mother.

My brother Manuel, who is now home, stares out the window with a blank face, no grimace, and no reaction. He seems to be elsewhere. He shows neither concern nor joy. He just stares. I feel like he's going to run out and will want to stay behind just to defy Papá. He doesn't say anything, so I don't know how he feels. He usually keeps to himself. I do

17

remember Papá saying that he moved here with them from Mexico, and maybe he doesn't want to go back to that. But Manuel doesn't let on.

The six of us will make the trip. It is Papá, my Mamá Angelita, two uncles, my brother and me.

My mother isn't around any more. Her name was Petra. Papá said that she died when I was four months old; she was only 27. No one ever talks about her, but I'd like to know what happened to her. I miss her even though I've never met her. All I hear is that she had problems after my birth. She died of liver and kidney failure and her body swelled up from storing toxic fluids that her organs couldn't expel. Why did she have to die? I didn't get to see her, yet I feel sad for her and miss her. I want to hug her just once. Did she love me?

Two toddler brothers, Creciano and Wilfredo, also died a year apart before I came along. Of course, I would have liked to have met them, too.

Maybe my mother died of sadness after my first two brothers died. No one talks about them either. My heart pounds when I think of how she helped me be born, and how I long to meet her, but I never will. I know she wouldn't have left me as if she didn't love me. She went through pain for me. Why did I live and not her? I will never know what it was like for her to have three babies, and only one lived. I will always think of her, and I would like to prove to her that I would have been a good son if she were here, just like I will be for Papá.

As if reading my mind, Papá walks over to me and rubs my head. I lean against his leg. I wish I could hug him, but he's so tall and I don't want him to hear my throat swallowing hard if he picks me up. I'm too old now for that, anyway.

The next couple of days, the men go back to work. On the night after that, we all pack our few things around the over-crowded three-room shack without a word. My two uncles will share a burlap sack for their belongings and then Papá and Mamá Angelita will share another for theirs. My brother and I get a small flour sack to put our clothes in. My shoes are worn, too tight and they hurt. They are too small. Mamá Angelita notices and tells me to leave them behind. But she immediately changes her mind. The next morning I will put them on because I have no others. I have one thing in my pocket: it's a smooth stone that I picked up on my way to school one day. It's a two-tone light brown stone with gold sparkles in layers. I like the way it shines and the hard surface with soft in between. I have heard Papá talk about finding small pieces of gold where he used to live in Mexico. The stone makes me think good things.

Mamá Angelita finishes packing some bean burritos, coffee and water for our trip, and keeps some cups handy. Her final task is to carefully arrange her little tin sewing box.

"Papá, do you think there is gold in my stone?" I hold it up toward his face and ask hopefully. He said that gold comes from rocks. People who have gold can probably buy lots of food and other needs without worrying, he said, even piñatas. We eat beans and tortillas.

"No, mijo (my son), I don't think so," he says without looking at it. I stand on my tiptoes and put it up higher to his face. He takes it from me. I see his tall silhouette standing in front of the window, with the kerosene lamp behind him. He looks at the stone for a long time. I can tell he is thinking about

19

something else. He hands it back without saying more. I walk away.

I know something is very wrong and I only feel safe with Papá. I'm not sure what will happen with me and I don't know the impact it will have on my life.

I lay down on my cot on the porch that night looking out toward a clear starry sky; an Arizona sky I am familiar with. My eyes blur a little. I see the Big Dipper and the Little Dipper that Papá has taught me to find. I outline them with my finger. They are just part of a family that sticks together, he said. Asterisms, he called them, and the sky is so large that they are just a small part of the whole sky. I also see a bright light coming from planet Venus nearby and right above me. It fits perfectly where a large hole has gotten bigger in the porch roof. I put my index finger and thumb together up to my eye and make a small circle. It makes the stars come into focus. I can almost touch them.

I wish upon a star someday I will know as much as Papá does.

Here I am, lost in space, not knowing where I will be in a couple of days. Wherever we go, I am sure we will see some stars. I have always asked a lot of questions about everything and Papá always has the answer. But earlier, seeing Papá's face, I didn't know what to ask. Now I'm lost.

In three mornings we will be on our way to the motherland – back to Mexico, where my family came from. At the word of two Americans in uniform, I learned that we are being kicked out of this country, and I now will fear the law. My brother is the only one who speaks English and he was not home to help. My family offered no excuses that might incense the officers to cause us difficulties. Papá said why argue? He knows the truth about who is and who isn't a U.S. citizen, and he doesn't need more problems.

Leaving Gilbert:

I don't know what time it is this morning but it is still dark outside. The only transportation in the area is by horse-drawn, covered wagons, or if you own a car. Until yesterday, Papá got up at 4:00 o'clock every morning and walked to the Pine Farm to work. There are no roads, only paths worn down by worn shoes and mostly tattered wagons. Sometimes one will go by and pick him up on the way to the Pine Ranch. It seems like they all work at the same ranch and say nice things about Mr. Pine. I just don't know where it is, but we are near the airport and I watch small airplanes go by daily.

We are outside waiting and a car comes by to pick us up. Eight other cars are behind it. Papá puts our sacks into the trunk and the six of us stuff ourselves in, with my brother and Papá, Manuel and me in the front seat with the driver. Mamá Angelita sits with my uncles in the back seat and is holding the bag with food in her lap.

I guess the same thing has happened to the others who are coming with us. If there are kids in there, I'm hoping I will find a friend one day. I am glad we are not the only ones making this trip.

I don't know if Papá is thinking of my mother, but we are leaving her behind somewhere in a cemetery. I never went to visit her. It makes me sad that I only have my grandmother to talk to. She asks questions, I answer, and then she usually says a final thing; "Youn'tand?" I don't know what that means but I nod my head in approval every time.

Our car heads south toward Mexico, 120 miles away to Nogales, Sonora. Papá says it is the nearest town just on the other side of the U.S./Mexico international border. He could have shown the officers his permanent resident green card, which would have been enough for him to remain in the U.S., and he could have stayed. But what would have happened to the rest of us? Does that mean I don't have to go to Mexico?

No one else in the family has any documents, he says, and he doesn't have any on-hand for me. Since my mother passed away he didn't know where to get them. So we will all stay together and we'll make it. The most important thing we will ever have is each other, he says.

"Manuel, are you going to miss school?" I ask my brother trying to think of something else to say. I look into his eyes, sitting next to me, and he looks like he's not there. He doesn't even look out the window.

"Do you think the kids will notice you're gone?" I prompt him again, hoping he says yes because then it will mean they might miss me too. They probably won't remember me, though. I think I was not there the day they took pictures.

He finally shrugs his shoulders without looking at me. I will think of the kids and remember their names because school is the only thing I had, but now it's gone. No one knows me. I don't know me.

Three days ago was the last of the occasional days when I showed up at school, a total of 16 days this year, Papá said.

The other reason I went to the Mexican School for only a few days is because I have to stay and help Mamá Angelita at home. She doesn't like me walking the two miles to or from school by myself.

When Manuel allows me to go with him, he's not reliable in returning with me, she tells him all the time. Living here for seven years does not mean I'll be safe by myself, she says. I am just in first grade.

But now school is out of my life. My education will have to wait.

When I look at Papá in the car, he is looking out the window. I think of how sad he must be for us to be thrown out of our home so quickly. What could he have done that is so bad to get rid of him in three days? Is he hiding something from us? What about my uncles? How can the officers just tell us to leave and we leave? I want to stay and go to school! But we must be guilty if they are kicking us out of the country.

Papá is leaving behind the only thing he can claim as part of his identity. His job. He is the boss in our home. He makes decisions. And he chooses to leave? I may not know why for a long time, but I'm going to try to find out.

He is keeping his eyes to the window. He's usually quiet, but now he's saying nothing. I think I know what he's feeling about having to leave, because I won't have a school to go to any more and I feel sad. My grandmother often looks at him for answers. He is a father left without a home, with two children, a family to support, and no job. How will he get us through this?

As we leave at dawn, I look back a final time and I see our dark, empty little shack in the moonlight for the very last time.

CHAPTER 3

Migrant Field Raids
1930

The Great Depression hits in the U.S. between 1929 and 1932, lasting long enough to the detriment of many people's living conditions.

With only a third-grade education, Papá tries to explain to us what is happening. It is the Stock Market crash, something he says he knows nothing of – but in my eyes there is nothing he doesn't know. He tells us that things have changed; rich people have lost businesses and a lot of money. That affects us too.

Farmers have produced and harvested too many crops, materials are in great supply, and no one is buying them because money has lost its value. The poor want to work, but because so much has already been produced for sale, there is no reason or money to continue to pay workers to produce more of the same things. Everything is stagnant.

Some states have been wiped out from torrential rains or dust storms. The government can no longer afford to give money to aid farmers losing their farms and crops to make up for their losses, as in the past. Now, neither Papá nor my uncles have jobs, so we have to start a new life back in Mexico.

Even poor gringos, Papá heard, are not welcome in other states. Mexican migrant workers have taken the back-breaking, low-paying jobs of working the fields, and now states fear that those from other areas will come and take those jobs at lower wages than locals. Due to need of more jobs, at this time the country is re-enforcing its immigration laws by knowingly and unknowingly deporting many U.S. and non-U.S. citizens to their countries of origin.

Those in authority force some of those actions illegally, mostly Immigration and Naturalization Services Border Patrol, deporting them based on their presumption that they are not American citizens.

Some of the private corporations and car companies are among those pushing to enforce this action, which is not a U.S. law and is in violation of civil rights.

A term that becomes common-place nationally and is being enforced as law is the wrongly-understood and non-existent repatriation act. There is no such Federal act. It does not exist and is not legislation. It should not be imposed on anyone because it is unconstitutional and illegal deportation of people.

Repatriation ordinarily implies a voluntary desire by someone to leave the country; it is not applied or coerced on someone.

In fact, several forces have come together to expel Hispanics from the country, and use them as scapegoats for officials' claimed intent to protect the rights of U.S. citizens. There is no due process for deported Hispanics and, "if individuals asked for a formal hearing and were denied entry, they were automatically barred from ever being able to enter the United States." It is a losing proposition all around for the deported. The racial tension weighs heavy on those being affected.

Whether it is our lack of knowing the language, our condition of being poor, our color, or our disposition that give us away, deportation happens more easily for us because of those reasons. And Papá says he heard that more than one million people of Hispanic descent, but at least 60 percent believed to be American born, are being deported from the U.S.

Many are taken via train and dropped off at the border, others get lost in the processing – which is not happening ethically or in a court of law. Some of those people suffering with tuberculosis, paralysis and other medical conditions are deported unconstitutionally against their will.

Immigration raids are taking place to find and expel mostly people of Hispanic descent, much of it done with aggression and with authorities overstepping their power.

I suddenly think of the condescending officer at our front porch with the smirk on his face when he left us at our shack. But the other guy was nice.

The overwhelming belief in the country seems to be that we should be escorted out of the territory, threatening and shaming most of those here legally or illegally into leaving before being ejected. The ones living here legally remain fearful of the system.

Papá tells me that one of my uncles, Epifanio, left the country "voluntarily" with his family only weeks earlier because he knew the raids were starting. But there are also distant relatives who stay behind earning extra money before their time comes. Some often stay permanently when they can and may never be discovered as being illegal. It is a draw between being lucky and being at the wrong place at the wrong time.

Word of mouth is that illegals are picked up and sometimes held in jails. They are sometimes taken by train or escorted to prisons or border cities elsewhere, far away from their original point of entry to disorient and discourage them from returning. Many get lost and start lives wherever they land, because it's too difficult to get back to their hometowns.

Families do not get to say goodbye and often don't know where their loved ones end up. News outlets through the years have reported stories of similar acts under various administrations, most notably starting with President Herbert Hoover during the Great Depression in 1929, including inexplicably separating children from parents.

"We were *invited to leave* the country," Papá explains in Spanish in the old car, "so we have to leave because the government thinks we are taking less pay for agricultural jobs that Americans can be doing. We are going back to Mexico to live."

To make it as a migrant, you have to be a hard worker, a cotton... melon... potato... tomato... or grape picker, construction worker, and janitor – whatever you can manage to do if your back can hold out. In the fields, a good straw hat is an unspoken requirement to protect them from the unforgiving sun. I have watched my father pick cotton and he is the fastest one in the field. Mamá

27

Angelita sometimes sends me out to the field on hotter days to take him and other workers some water to drink. I carry a 20-pound metal bucket-full of water from the cleaner part of the running canal nearby that she boiled earlier. Sometimes I spill more than I deliver, with the bucket splashing from one leg to the other, holding the handle tightly as I walk. They understand. Some water is better than none.

They each could toil up to 10-hour days either by the pound, or for $2 a day total if they picked more than per pound. Papá is impressed with his niece Marina, who is a faster worker than he is. She is always one of the first to take her bags filled to the top with cotton to a place where they are weighed and are given a slip of paper with the weight of cotton picked to turn in until payday.

Some workers are given much bigger lots than others to harvest because of their speed, and at times creates stress among them because they consider it an unfair employment environment.

It doesn't matter how productive they are, the chance exists daily that they can be sent back to their country. When the officers suddenly show up on their surprise raids, "La Migra! La Migra!" resonates like the wind through the acreage and through the crops. The men throw themselves onto the ground in hopes of not being spotted. Some crawl out of there quickly. La Migra usually picks up the front guys and throw all the ones they can into vans and take them to jail.

Papá was safe – until now. He said when some of the laborers are picked up, they never get paid. Who knows how many times that happened, to the benefit of the employer? And who knows which unethical employer may have called La Migra on a Friday?

"In the fields you are made to obey, not question authority," Papá would tell all the workers. "And even if you don't question them, you are here illegally, so you can go at any time." And now he is telling us that most don't have a chance to say goodbye to family, to let them know where they are or will be. They themselves don't know.

"La Migra has the right to do anything they want to us," Papá said to us matter-of-factly." Resigned to fate, he finished, "You don't mess with the law."

I imagine us all in jail behind black metal bars.

"Papá, how will I find you if they put us in jail!" my voice squeaks out as a shrill panicked sound. I look at his eyes for relief.

His quiet demeanor makes me wonder if he really believes they can do anything to us, but my respect for authority comes from his voice and that exchange. I've never seen Papá over-react; his actions are always right.

"They won't put us in jail because we are leaving," he answers. I am relieved to hear it.

The green uniforms are the U.S. Immigration Officers, Papá says, called "La Migra" for short. That's what everyone calls them. Out here where we live, those words are well known but I didn't know who they were until now.

Word travels at the speed of lightning when La Migra is approaching. They notify each other of the threat with a "La Migra!" yell and pass it on down the irrigation ditches, or do bird calls by rolling the tongue onto the bottom of the top teeth and making a trrrrrr vibrating sound. It is loud enough that it can be heard through any crop or barrier in the fields. When La Migra is nearing for a raid to pick up presumed non-US citizens, our job is to avoid them, but never to run once they spot you.

Everyone is afraid that La Migra will send us to the other side. Wherever that is, or wherever we go, I hope I will be with Papá. I've never been to Mexico. It could be a nice experience.

Like many others who headed north *from* Mexico years ago to try to make a better living, my father and his family were part of those who had entered the country, four illegally, years earlier. The U.S. is a place I will covet because it sounds like a better place than the one we're going to. I keep wondering why Papá would want to stay in a place where we aren't wanted.

"Manuel!" my usually calm grandmother sighs and speaks to Papá in a husky whisper in the car. "What do we do now? How and where will we live? There is no opportunity in Mexico. That's why we left!" Her Spanish becomes more accentuated and high pitched as she hangs onto the seat, resisting leaving.

Papá says he doesn't know where we will land. If he doesn't know, and he's the smartest one, I'm scared. But he knows we will need those $2 a day to make it. Nogales, Sonora, MX, is the closest place we can go and we will find work. He has been a miner and has moved around looking from town to town in Mexico – through lowlands and up the mountains. He's not afraid.

Another country sounds so far away to me, strange and scary. But here we are now – moving forward.

I try to imagine another way of living from what I know – but I really can't since I have never been away from the rural road I lived on in Arizona.

"Papá, what is Nogales like? Will I have friends there?" I ask hoping to cheer him up while he stares straight ahead. There were only a couple of kids like me where we lived, but they seldom came outside. Now I think I know why.

Papá tells me that Nogales is a two-entry border city where gringos like to cross to party hard, drink lots of tequila and visit women friends. He knows what awaits us. It does not sound like something he looks forward to and neither do I.

CHAPTER 4

Deportation to Mexico
1930

Entering Nogales, Sonora, MX.

It is early morning and I wake up rubbing my eyes. It's my first ride in a car and I can't believe we are still in it. I sit up and see several booths with border police looking inside car windows, talking to the drivers. Ours tells them we are coming back to stay. One officer looks through the bags in the trunk, and then reaches for Mamá Angelita's food bag. She hangs onto it with both hands and for a second I think he is going to take it. Then the officer changes his mind and waives us through past the station.

"We just crossed the border station into Mexico, mijo," he says. "This is Nogales, where we will live." He never loses patience with me. My eyes finally clear up just as the driver pulls over.

The car drops us off in the middle of the main street. I think we lost contact with the cars that were following us. It is very different here from where I lived just yesterday. We walk down the street with our bags and I don't know where we're going. But I trust Papá.

Vendors stand outside their small 4' x 6' hole-in-the-wall stores. They are trying to woo customers in.

"We have it right here, Mister! Whatever you're looking for, gifts, piñatas, tequila, and whiskey! We have lots of whiskey! We have jewelry, refreshments, food, and cold drinks. We have everything, Miss!"

As we walk down the street, almost every other vendor repeats the same line over and over, as if they have all those items. It's in choppy, accentuated English, but they all seem to have memorized those twenty words and yell them out to anyone passing by. I hold Papá's hand and watch some drunken gringos trying to buy several bottles of alcohol. They want a discount for buying several bottles and the owner won't agree on a price. He finally gives in and the people walk away happy.

"Some money is better than no money," says Papá.

I think that he is very smart with mathematics and maybe he can should a job down here. I tell him that, but he doesn't think so.

My father is a miner by trade. He drills holes with a special instrument by hand into the mountain-side and then attaches large tie-down hardware into the rock. He is skilled but with no type of his work available, and no money, Papá and his brothers have to look farther. Full-time employment is almost unheard of, and they will labor by day wherever they can.

He talks to some people on the street asking for a place to rent, but no one knows of any. He finds a former female companion with two of her own small children he used to live with here. He had left her behind when he moved to the other side of the U.S. border to work, not knowing where their relationship stood.

He had gotten a message to her letting her know we were returning and asked her if she had some space for us to stay until he found a job. Only if it is necessary, he said. And that's how it worked out.

There's a small cast-iron stove in a corner, a dilapidated table that is literally on its last original leg. The three other corners rest on pieces of wood that have been nailed into the tabletop. It leans against the wall. A couch sits nearby, looking like it was pulled from a pile someone left behind. We certainly don't have a right to judge or complain. There's a roof over our heads. Then we walk into a small bedroom with three beds and two boxes with clothes nearby. Papá looks at us and says we'll have to make it here with them, now a total of nine people.

As the days go by, we live one meal at a time. I don't know where or how the woman gets any support but I am grateful for it. She looks mean and her tone is demeaning. She obviously does not want company. But what choice does Papá have now? With him not finding a job quickly, I realize I have never been this hungry. I can't deny that I would like more food.

When he works, he stops to buy beef at the butcher's where it is hung out to dry. It's as if the flies follow the smell of the meat the whole way home. The angry woman doesn't like to cook, she says. So Mamá Angelita always washes the meat down with a little water from the container. I can see she takes pleasure in cooking for us, probably grateful we have food. She covers it with sackcloth. She tries to get the fire going on the stove for when Papá arrives. It takes a while because she has to go find wood. After waiting for food, it's easy to forget the flies were on the meat.

This day Papá brings beans *and* meat. At times Mamá Angelita is able to make another whole meal out of small leftovers with bones that give the soup great flavor. Her "caldo" is the best, a stew with a large bone, small pieces of potatoes, carrots, and corn on the cob, if we have it. Otherwise, it is just a broth with thick flavor and tortillas, the Lord's daily bread. She has always made them; the smell makes me run in and ask for one. She gladly complies. I hug her and she tells me she loves to see me happy. I love seeing her toothless smile and gray hair in a bun.

Papá gets home tired of walking up and down the street, day in and day out, asking people for work. I want so much to be helpful.

"Papá, will you please let me go with you?" I beg him every morning. "I know what to do. I can help you!"

"And who will stay to watch over your grandmother?" we say it in unison. I know. It's

34

always the same question to my question. Then he rubs my head and walks out the door. I like him rubbing my head. But I would like to hug him.

I don't know why Papá's companion, that's what he calls her, doesn't like me. I think I am a decent human being and very well behaved. I am not sure of my relationship to her, but I don't want to get close to her. Contrary to Papá, she never has a good word for anyone. She makes my brother Manuel and me sleep on the cold floor that she sprays with water every night before we lay down. Anyone with a brain knows it is colder that way, even if it's summer time, so she can't blame ignorance. I feel it is deliberate. We manage on our small blanket. I would rather put the blanket under me than over me. Manuel wants it over him, so we fix it just right. When she makes a meal, she gives both of her sons the meat portions and usually gives my brother and me the broth of the soup. At least we are getting to eat. Mamá Angelita seems to do okay without much food.

Papá cannot be blind to it, but he is gone a lot and I will not tell him how she acts. To help out, the wicked woman makes tortillas and I sell them door-to-door. I am good in math so I am never cheated. But sometimes older guys rob me on the streets. I sew a small pocket inside the front of the band of the waist in my pants and I learn to hide the occasional bills in there. When they shake me down they can't find it. They take the change and run. Then they start taking the tortillas. When I am short of money or tortillas, I fear going home to explain to the grouch. I never steal. She never believes that I didn't take money or tortillas and there is no way to convince her or make it up to her. She hits me on the head in a side-swipe slap, regardless of the situation. At one point I realize that my own brother Manuel, who has been short of height, and overweight since a young age, has been eating many of the tortillas and I was getting punished! When I tell him, he never fesses up to it, obviously not seeing the need for it. I don't like it but I semi-smirk to myself at his deceptive and distressing antics. I wish I'd had the courage to eat the tortillas since I am hungry and I am being punished for the missing ones he's taking! Whenever the lady is around, there is no winning for me. There are many incidents where I am neither at fault nor have I done anything to deserve her hatred or berating me.

I have few things to complain about in life and have never wished anyone bad, but my silent hope for this woman is that the Lord might hold a long, strong flame to her feet as judgment. That's how much physical and emotional pain I feel coming from her.

I am a good kid and don't cause any trouble. Knowing Papá's expectations and standards for keeping values and high morals, I know I will never steal food or anything else. I am not so sure about my brother Manuel, who is a fast talker – in English or Spanish. He is not quite so virtuous. I can hear my father get after him sometimes, but I don't spend much time with him. I never know what he is doing out of my father's watchful eye, which is often.

Back in School:

Once we settle in Nogales, I am happy to go back to elementary school. I start first grade again because I attended only a few days of school in Gilbert. This teacher is not good with her students. She seems to always be irritated at someone but takes it out on us kids. She is a large size and overweight physically, and she hits students on the head with a ruler. I don't see the reason. She does it much more often than she should; she walks by and whacks someone on the head or pulls their ear. It's a bad image for a teacher, whom I think is supposed to be there to help us. Many call her the "Monster." I don't like being in her classroom, even though she's never hit me. I feel lucky to lay low, be quiet and answer only if prompted by the ruler pointing at me.

Going into the second year, I am one of three students that always seem to have the answers when prompted with the pointing of a ruler. I am very proud of myself and stand up quickly next to my desk when they point at me calling me by name, "Fernando, Señor?" I can see the instructor is encouraged and satisfied by correct responses. It's easy for me in Spanish to do well in mathematics, history and reading. I also do well on tests.

I am delighted to be learning every subject. The manner in which most teachers and parents address pupils and vice versa is respectful, using the titles of "Señor" (Sir) or "Señorita" (Miss). There is no disobedience or you are sent to the principal's office. Seldom is there a second offense.

"Fernando, please come up here, Señor," my second-grade teacher says to me one day from the front of the room. I stand next to my desk immediately. I like her being my teacher. Her name is Lupe Vejar Varela.

This is the year I find out I am poor. And while the kids may not remember me when I leave, they will remember that my family did not have much and I had to get free-meal tickets. It changes my perspective on life.

This year still turns out to be really good and I learn a lot. I retain so much of the information and that teacher is so much better. She is fair with all the children. My third grade also turns out to be a great year. I will remember those two teachers often. But I will also remember that I did not return to school.

The move for Mamá Angelita:

We have been in Nogales for close to three years and I have loved my classes the whole time. Mamá Angelita is very ill. Home remedies are common but they don't always work. You can't just run to a doctor or have them make a house call if you don't have the money. Mamá Angelita seems to know she's getting close to the end.

"Manuel, I want to be buried at the top of the hill in Rosarito, where I was born," she says to Papá. "And I want to be near "La Lluvia" (the Rain), where I've always wanted to return. I know we don't have the money but I hope we can make it there before I die," that is her wish.

She always speaks of La Lluvia as if she has a love of it. Papá occasionally mentions it too. He explains that it is the "Lluvia de Oro," (the Rain of Gold), a mine where some people experienced a windfall from it in the early 1900's. Maybe that is another reason for returning. But they don't really remember how to get to it and it's not that close to her hometown. I think, maybe it's just a thing they remember as being prosperous and, with our situation, still hope to find.

My father wants to keep his promise to Mamá Angelita to put her to rest near her homeland near San Jose de Gracia in Mexico. It's far away and how will we get there without a car, I wonder. If we take the train, Papá says it's 942km, 585 miles. It would take more than 20 hours by car, if one goes the shortest route, but not all those roads are in driving condition. And if we walk it'll take many times longer. I don't know if we'll ever get there.

After providing shelter and meals, somehow Papá is able to save or get enough money for us all to leave on our search for an unknown future.

"Work is finished here. We will be leaving tomorrow by train," he tells us one day. It reminds me of when we left Gilbert overnight. But this time we'll be ready.

I eventually figured out that we had no "home" in Gilbert. That little place wasn't ours. But I came to love it and now miss our little cottage back there. It was a sure place to come home to. Not living anywhere too long is probably the reason I do not feel uprooted when we move again.

It is April. I have turned 10 years old. We have no celebrations for birthdays in our family, but it's not a problem for me. Piñatas don't matter. Mamá Angelita gives me two warm tortillas with butter at the table. Once I find out that we are leaving, I ask if I can stay behind because I want to go to school. It is the place I feel most at home, where I know what to expect. Of course, I realize as soon as I say it that I can't stay behind because there's no one to leave me with. I don't want to hear that I will not get to attend classes any more.

I'm afraid I won't be returning, ever. The kids will remember that I was a poor kid and that I got a meal ticket. I will remember that I don't want to mock anyone for anything.

I wonder again if they will miss me.

Leaving by Train:

I jump out of my cot this morning thinking about being on board a train; hearing the horn and engine sounds when it takes off.

I have never been on a train! We live very close to the station and sometimes I stand outside waiting for it to come by. Today I will be on it! I tell Papá maybe the driver knows me because I usually waive at him.

"Conductor," Papá corrects me. "The driver is called a train conductor." I am excited and anxious to know what the train ride will be like.

My father doesn't tell us where we are going but we trust him. Maybe he doesn't know yet himself. We are prepared to leave that morning toward the next state of Sinaloa, he says, into the deep terrain of Mexico. I wonder if the train goes through the mountains, or what if we have to walk through them?

I don't understand how Mamá Angelita can pack overnight! I find out that she has to leave some small things behind. But I know she will never leave her embroidery box containing used and reused sewing thread for what she considers her works of art. Small kitchen towels, doilies; those are her treasures of love; she gifts friends with them.

"Mijo, did you get the small box behind the door? Youn'tand? That little box I asked you to bring?" she asks me finally sitting down as the train is taking off. "Youn'tand?" she says while she nods. I think I'm supposed to also, so I nod back.

My green eyes suddenly feel bloodshot and get as big as marbles. I am so eager to be leaving on the train that I am sitting there acting like I'm driving it! I feel my face burning red and my brow wrinkle deepening. I can't answer. I have forgotten the only thing I am responsible for. We can't go back for it. I feel bad for Mamá Angelita and want to cry.

She never tells me she is upset but she looks sad. I can see she will miss her few things. If we move somewhere else, I promise myself that I will always look around to make sure I don't forget anything. I see a full set of gums in her half-smile. She's so kind to me. The only thing that makes me feel better is the smooth stone in my pocket. With yesterday's pants on, it's bound to be there.

CHAPTER 5

Deeper South
1933

By the time we leave Nogales by train, Manuel is 15 and he seems to think he is all grown-up. He wants his independence so he tells Papá he is staying behind. He decides that because he speaks broken English, foreign to the locals, and they make fun of him, calling him a "pocho," he will stay close to the border. Mexicans usually refer to a pocho as a person who has somehow betrayed his heritage and taken on the American way of life. They may not speak either language well so they don't feel they belong in either place. In Manuel's case, he has been living in the U.S. with us those seven years, since I was born. He lived in Mexico the previous five years with family. He doesn't want to go to a new place now and face the same thing. My uncles also decide to stay and continue working small jobs.

We head out toward the state of Sinaloa, Mexico, Mamá Angelita's place of birth, to comply with her wishes. Papá remains involved with his female companion and she wants to come with us, and bring her two children. We are living with them in this small space. Papá tells her it's not a good idea because we will have hardship and it will be difficult for the little ones. He does not want to bring them along and I'm glad because my dislike for her is more than I've ever felt. Maybe Papá has seen her mean-spirited ways of dealing with my brother and me. My brother can usually slip out without a problem, but I have to stay behind and deal with the hate on her lips. I don't say anything bad about her. He has enough to deal with.

Mamá Angelita can't stand her and they exchanged harsh words one time. But the woman is still able to convince my father that she and her children need to go with us because her mother lives where we are going.

"Papá, I love the train, don't you?" I ask him every time I hear the horn grow louder as we get closer to any small town. The train blows large puffs of smoke at these points. We are warning people to get out of the way. They come out to wave and see the train inching by like a caterpillar. I wave back. I am lucky to be on it!

"Can we stay on it forever?" I ask hopefully. "I'm going to be a train driver when I grow up!" I say in a commanding voice.

"Conductor", he corrects me again. "You have to go to school for that and I don't think you'll be able to go." School has been left behind for me, and I don't expect to return.

The train ride is the best time of my life! I am in my own world and it is bliss! The wind blows our hair. Mamá Angelita has packed some egg and bean burritos for us and it feels great to eat on the train. It's like the picnic I enjoyed with her outside one time while we waited for Papá.

I point things out to them. We occasionally hear running water in creeks nearby. When the engine quiets down we hear the sounds of wildlife howling. The fresh air from the top of the mountains really wakes us up. I will not forget this trip ever; these beautiful mountains, the colors of the trees, flowers and creeks. And then we end up in Hermosillo, which will take us toward our destination.

My First Paying Job at Camp Wilson, Bamoa:

We have now gone further south past the big Hermosillo via railroad. We are arriving at the next train station in Bamoa, Sonora, about a 400-mile trek south of the border.

I cannot believe my luck! Something else happens to me at the next train stop! Arriving at a Camp Wilson nearby, I get my first job picking cotton.

I am elated to be so far away and to finally get a job at the age of 10. I know it has more to do with my having grown taller and maybe they think I'm older.

I'll finally have a chance to show Papá that I can do it. I've watched his skill and effort in 100-degree weather long enough, and I am sure I can do it, too. I am a lot closer to the ground and my back can take it much more easily. I would take his place if I could. I am growing up fast and it feels great to be productive and be paid for it. He said we are staying here for a few weeks till work runs out and I learn how to harvest my first crop.

My pride is obvious to Papá after some time of making myself useful. I gladly hand him my money to help out. It is a small assignment completed for a short period of time.

"Papá, I told you I could help you. They should have given me a job before now. Maybe you could take a break, or quit working so hard," I tell him. I am serious but he just bows his head up and down and smiles, as if I'm right.

Our business is done and we are ready to move on. However, I can tell he has a serious concern. I see it in his deep wrinkle. I want to be the last reason for any problem he may have.

Mamá Angelita:

Papá notices that Mamá Angelita has been keeping up with us to this point, but she is losing weight and having a hard time with hot weather, nutrition and walking. She has become seriously sick and we are lacking medical care for her along the way. As we approach our destination of San Jose de Gracia, Papá decides that she is too weak to walk the rest of the trip. At the next town Papá arranges what he can to help her along, and offers to pay four men to transport her for about 65 miles via a home-made stretcher he put together. She is 90 years old and she is worn out. There's nothing that will prevent Mamá Angelita's nearing demise.

We all walk along the dirt trails near the Sinaloa River. That river would have been a great refuge for us, if it were not dry.

When we arrive, distant relatives offer us lodging until we get settled. Papá finds a job and I help him as much as I can. I also run errands for Mamá Angelita's medicines, but her health worsens.

A doctor is called in, but she does not improve. Everyone talks about her condition, some visit her and the town ladies pray their rosaries for her every single night at the house.

A couple of weeks later, almost as if she has any control over her living, she calls Papá and me to her bedside. That morning she blesses us and, as we hug her, she takes a deep breath. It is her last. Papá tells me we are lucky to be in her presence and that she just died. We are saddened to see her go. We stand and watch her for a while and we are glad we talked to her before she went. A priest is standing by giving her last rites. Her wish to be buried at the top of the hill at Rosarito nearby will be granted. She also wanted to buy me some shoes, so Papá does that next day and I get to wear them to her funeral.

It is a simple ceremony in the house where we are staying. She lays un-embalmed in the casket and it should be a quick funeral because the body can't be kept in the house too long. The smell will be unbearable in a couple of days. Her body takes up the majority of the living room. A priest comes to bless her. A few ladies in black clothes stand in the tiny room praying for her, asking the Lord to take her soul to Heaven. I can't understand a lot of what they say because it's the same thing over and over.

I finally get the nerve to go up close to look at her lying in a casket. Her small hands are cold and they hold her beloved prayer beads in them. After a while I touch her fingers and they tightly hold her piece of faith. I believe she'll never let it go. She's so cold I want to put a blanket on her. I run my hand across her forehead. She has wrinkles and looks tired. It seems like things happen and I want to cry, but I can't. Papá comes and stands next to me. He puts his arm around me and I hide my face in his waistline. We both go back and sit down, and his sturdy arm around me makes me feel strong.

The next morning I vividly recall her casket being carried up a hill with a few people making the short walk to the top. This is her cherished Rosarito, where she wants to be. A priest blesses her a final time.

Right beside her grave, I place a small sewing box I made from tiny boards and nailed them with a rock. I filled it with small trinkets. I put in it a stick with pieces of thread wrapped around it, a spool I had found and cleaned up, a broken piece of chain and a dried yellow daisy flower. I pulled my smooth brown and gold-colored stone out of my pocket and put it inside the box.

And then I cry.

I suddenly remember the word she used to say to me all the time. "Youn'tand?" I did not know what it meant then but I started saying it to myself over and over. Youn'tand? Youn'tand? But I don't understand and I shake my head no, no, no. I will miss her.

My father is standing next to me and his eyes well up with tears when I look up at him. I wonder if this is the way it was with my mother when she died. I am glad I wasn't there to see it. I miss her more and wish she were here with me now.

As we walk back down the hill, I wipe the dust off my shoes with my hand. I take care of them like Papá does his hat. Mamá Angelita would have been so happy to see my shoes. I then remember La Lluvia de Oro where she wanted to go. We did not make it there.

Within the next month, Papá gets a few different jobs doing what he can. Our time in San Jose de Gracia goes by quickly and he wants to move on. Without Mamá Angelita, now he has one less person to worry about. The best news for both of us is when his companion tells him she is staying behind with her mother! That is the best feeling for me in a long time; and I sense the same from Papá even though he doesn't say it.

He tells me he has gotten that unforgettable obsession to go back North again, and to pursue his legal residency for employment in North America. I am glad he is finally making his attempt to return.

Heading Out:

Papá has developed a good relationship with a man who picks cotton with him. They usually sit out in the field in shaded areas and talk for long whiles. It seems this is one of the first friendships Papá has established.

A couple of months after our arrival in San Jose de Gracia, Papá mentions that we are ready to leave. He asks his friend if we can borrow his donkey to carry our belongings on our trip north. His name is El Bonito (The Pretty One). Business is done on a handshake and both men know they may never see each other again, or money may not be exchanged, but trust is the highest honor. Papá gives him a few pesos and they agree to square up at a later time. I wonder when or if Papá will be able to pay him back.

We are prepared to leave the next day and plan to take El Bonito. We pack up our few belongings, mostly food, and the man bids us farewell. It's nice of him to walk El Bonito with us out of town for about a half mile to say goodbye. That donkey is his best friend. It's sad for us to take him from his master, but glad to have some help carrying the bulk on his back.

This is the second trip this far south for Papá. I am sure it is taking longer on our return now through the mountains. I trek well with him and neither one of us needs to mention it. Temporary jobs get us through. His mind and burden are now lighter. He says we will go back to the land we were ejected from. I truly can't understand why we didn't stay.

My uncles and my brother went a different direction in life, who knows where they are. Mamá Angelita has passed away, and here we are now almost 500 miles from the border. I find no logical reason to be this far. It sounds like a difficult goal to go back. But I have to believe that it will happen because Papá believes it. I now want to make it my objective to help get us there. Our trip has just become easier by leaving four people behind. What do we have to lose?

Reaching small towns:

As we walk out past Yecorato, a farming area by the river, Papá instinctively leans over to pick a stem of cotton plant to ward off some dogs that are approaching us. As soon as he scares them off, he checks the plant for ripeness. A grand-motherly lady hobbles out of her house, almost running toward us with apron untied and a rolling pin in hand, yelling as we approach.

"Don't pick the cotton! I don't want anyone touching it. It'll ruin the crop!" she yells. We know it will not ruin the crop, but Papá has told me we all have country tales we believe.

I suddenly smell a home-made tortilla coming from her house. I want one so badly; if I can, I will ask her for one for Papá, one for El Bonito, and one for myself. How I wish Mamá Angelita was alive. "Youn'tand?" I thought to myself. I miss her and her tortillas.

"Stay here, let me talk to the woman," Papá says.

He approaches her and tells her he doesn't want her to lose the harvest, and he means it. With so much lack in our lives, Papá can't stand to see crops or anything else wasted. With just one look at the field, he figures out quickly what she can expect to pay us for picking the whole area. It turns out to be less than someone else has charged her in the past. I notice he says "us" and I'm so content that he's counting me in to help.

He negotiates with her for a fair amount that will benefit both parties. She hires us to pick the cotton and do other small tasks for several months. We stay on her land during that time and it's now easier to save money. Even El Bonito got to eat well enough here.

As we travel, I am restoring the names of all those places where we stop. It seems so different from what other people do compared to a normal town like Gilbert. There, Papá woke up at 4:00 a.m. and went to work each day. And now he has to go out and search where there is none. I hope one day I will be able to tell others what we did and the places we visited.

My trek through the miles we have walked awakens my senses. Being a naturalist at heart, my father teaches me many things he seems to know by experience. I learn about animals, their rituals and feeding habits, flora and their relationship to the air, sun, the water and us. Every day I feel more oriented as to the direction we are headed. Papá shows me how to estimate the time we will arrive. I can tell time very closely based on the sun's position. I love walking but, when I think of the distance, I feel tired.

The most enjoyable moments to me are when we talk into the night if we don't have to walk the next morning. I like spending time with him and learning more. I also like to talk to other people and see how they live. Our lodging throughout this trip has been interesting, although I know Papá does not like staying with others because he knows it's an inconvenience to them. I have never felt closer to anyone than him. Now we are back out in the wilderness.

One night during our fireside chat Papá tells me something I find a little strange. It's very unlike him. We talk for a longer time than usual about astronomy, the mystery of numbers to infinity, about the birds and the bees, and then women. He leans close to me, lowering his voice to share a private moment.

"A man needs a female companion," he explains, pausing for a long moment. I notice that he's been with a woman for a time wherever we go and it seems to be natural thing for him, but a taboo subject between us. Sometimes the women don't know about others. He is a good-looking light-skinned man, with blue eyes, about six feet tall. His Stetson hat is his trademark. In the evenings he wraps it up carefully before going to sleep. And I wrap up my belt and my shoes.

"A man needs a female companion," he starts out again. "But don't ever kill a man for the love of a woman," he says looking down. He appears to be in a state of misery. I begin to wonder why. Again, I hope that woman was my mother; and I hope he did not have to kill for her. He never mentions that again. When he doesn't explain things, I have to try to make meaning out of it. This time I'm not sure of the significance of this conversation, but I will follow his law.

I know little about him because he is somewhat serious about life and doesn't say much about himself. He is appropriate in his talks with me. He is a calm man and seldom raises or lowers his voice. He has never struck me. He only admonishes me with virtuous poems I have to figure out for myself. Moral Maxims, as he calls them.

"Fernandohhhh," is how he gets my attention when he wants me to listen up.

"Papáhhhh," I answer letting him know I heard him. He laughs. During those times of fellowship, he sings songs of women who hurt men in love. I have never seen him drink before but I wonder about his mood.

He labors hard and I like to see him smile and laugh, especially if it's at me. We stay on the move with the desire for better days.

Animals or rodents usually don't bother us; we just have to be aware of them coming too close. We avoid killing them, but there are a couple of snakes that come too close while we are walking.

"Can we cook snakes?" I ask when we come across one. "Somebody told me we can cook 'em."

"If you want to catch it, you can cook it. I won't," he chuckles. "And I wouldn't get close to a rattler. They rattle their tails to let you know they are close by, and their poison can kill you. Who will walk with me then?"

"I heard some people wear snake boots. We could eat some snake and save the rest to make you some shoes," I insist. "Can we make you some?"

"How big is the snake? Do you know how to make shoes?" Papá answers again laughing. He is irritating me because I'm trying to come up with ideas that will help us. He needs new shoes.

So we pass up on the snake. I am glad that we can keep shoes on our feet. Mine are like new but Papá still supplants the inside of his with cardboard.

El Fuerte:

Still in the state of Sinaloa, we go northwest, heading for the larger town of El Fuerte (The Fort, or The Strong One) to be there before sunset. It is about 30 miles from where we are toward the Gulf of California. It sounds close by and I can't wait to get there.

Papá says that El Fuerte is a very hot place with the large Rio Fuerte (Strong River) running through it. The humidity is unbearable.

"Papá, do you want to swim in the river when we get there? Do you remember when I jumped in a small creek and you had to pull me out? I'll make sure that does not happen again," I assure him.

"I suppose we could swim, if we knew how, but we don't," he chuckles at me. "And we also can't swim because even if we knew how, the current is too strong for us. But we can stand on the sidelines to wash up holding on to a rope tied to a tree. What do you think?"

"That'll be good, I think." I say bobbing my head, even though I still want to swim. As if reading my mind, he looks at me and tells me not to try it.

We a lot of fruit from trees and enjoy it with water under the shade of a tree. I am in charge of rationing what we have by coordinating the distance with our arrival at the next town. It's much easier with just the two of us. We also replace the insoles of his shoes with hard cardboard, covering new holes as they appear. Mine are getting better since I've broken them in but are also showing a little wear. I hope they last a long time. We don't have socks. We get small itchy sores just above the ankles and up the leg a short way, much like chigger bites. I am surprised we don't get blisters on our feet. Maybe they are too calloused. The bottoms hurt from walking, though.

"Papá," I ask on the way, trying to get a feel for his reception, as he looks down at me. "A friend said the ocean is in our direction. Since we're going that way, I want to see it. Can we go?"

He laughs as if I am joking. I say it again and he tells me he's never been there. And, he tells me, we're not on a vacation. And we don't have a car. The ocean is about 70 miles past the Rio Fuerte (River) where we're headed. Do I want to walk the extra miles?

I believe we deserve a vacation. But I think of our feet and that's the end of that conversation.

After a long walk with talk, we arrive in El Fuerte. We find a place to land and put some blankets on the ground right under a huge umbrella-top tree. It is nice and cool. At night we pick fruit to last a few days. We are happy to eat guavas, oranges and apples hanging from the trees at the base of the river. We eat them with gusto for all the meals we've missed. As Papá says:

"Panza llena, corazon contento!" That is, full tummy, happy heart again. I truly appreciate the meaning of that saying. Food and singing make us happy.

54

La Aduana – Church Shelter:

Populations in these villages are small so we have to make way for ourselves. There isn't enough work for both locals and us. I wake up daily with curiosity, never knowing where we're going. It has become our lifestyle.

We are back in the state of Sonora and I am feeling like we are making more progress as the days roll by. We find an old abandoned church in La Aduana, the nearest small town on our way.

Ordinarily, we get permission from the property-owners to squat on their land. Sometimes we sleep in deserted small sheds after we fully exert ourselves in the fields. I am helping more often. After a couple of months the church feels like our own home, something we haven't experienced in a while. It has become our refuge. Papá sings in the vacant building and the echo sounds clear and nice within the emptiness. I know all his songs, so I join him and the sound brings more harmony between us. I wish I had a harmonica. I would love to play one, even if I've never done so. I'm sure I can.

At times we walk to Alamos, about five miles away, so we can enjoy a very colorful populated church and plaza where the townspeople gather. El Bonito doesn't have to carry anything those days when he goes to experience some fun with us. He seems to enjoy people-watching as much as we do. What he does is get close to other donkeys when he can. They seem to be whispering to each other.

Enclosed buildings are such a blessing and protect us from the elements and mostly iguanas. We have to be careful with them, large lizards that look mean, because they love fruit and I won't let them get ours, that is for sure. They say there is water nearby when they are around.. We passed a river on the way here so I am sure there are many more close by. I am afraid of them but I call out to them, and Papá tells me to stay away because of their small sharp teeth. They eat only plants, but they can bite through my skin. They are fun to watch because they hang all over the trees and move so quickly that they appear to fly. Their colorful hard skin is like a snake's. They stand out and I usually spot them from far away. I do not get too close to them.

As if it were our home, having the church to stay in feels almost better than having shoes, as long as we're not walking. It is a luxury. It is so well built that I'm certain it will last for over a hundred years. Maybe one day I can come back and see it.

Papá's Life-Changing Accident: Minas Nuevas - Minitas 1935

Other than these small towns in between, it's been a long-distance trek with this nice break, but in a few weeks we are ready to hit the road again. Only a couple of miles away, Papá finds his next employment. We trudge northward to Minas Nuevas, a large group of mines. He begins work in one called Minitas.

Our only source of light has been by sun or lantern at night. Some of our best conversations take place under the moonlight and we save the kerosene for essential times. We carry it with us, ready for use.

Nearing the last days of our stay in Minitas, an accident happens. On a darker night when the sun is down and the moon is opaque, Papá is walking back to our shelter from the mine. It is about two miles from where we are staying, but close to other shelters so I am not alone when he works.

He knows the path, but it's 10:00 p.m. and he cannot see clearly where he is walking. His lantern runs out of kerosene about 600' from me. He steps into a cholla cactus that penetrates through his pant leg just on the right side of the shin.

No spiny cactus is fun to fall into, but this one is known as a jumping cactus. It has a tall trunk with lots of arms branching out to the sides, and lots of spiny needles coming from each. The thin spikes seem to jump out at you when walking by. They somehow show up on your body without you feeling them until a bit later. They stick into you and they are hard to remove without tugging on them.

Papá feels the pain starting but he has to make it to our shelter. He feels the sting more by the minute, worsening with every step. The needle feels as if it's digging deeper into him with every move. He does not try to pull his pant leg up as it might burrow the needle further in. Hoping not to run into another cactus, he makes it to our camping "home." When he gets there, he says he called out to me but I must not have heard him, even in the still of the night.

In the dark, he touches the needle poking out over his pant leg, and I watch his leg jerk. He pulls his pant leg up to the thorn slowly so as not to aggravate it. His leg is very swollen. He pulls on the cactus needle from outside the fabric and removes the sticker over it. He carefully nurses it for the next couple of days.

Papá cannot work and we leave after a few days. I notice that Papá is limping.

"Are you hurt, Papá? What is wrong with your leg?" I ask him, somewhat worried because I saw him limping yesterday when he stayed at our camp. He continues to walk, but I can see he is trying to ignore the pain.

He denies anything being wrong, probably because we have no way to pay for medical care. However, at the next town we find someone to look at his leg. The man who treats him appears to be somewhat of a medic that the people visit there. To my relief, he also seems to know what he's doing. Of course, he tells Papá what we already know – that he has a serious infection. He also says it comes from the sheath, likened to a sword cover, that goes over the cactus needle. Once the needle was removed, the sheath stayed inside his leg. So now we know. He cleanses the infection and tries to remove the sheath, but it won't come out. The heat and walking on it have made it worse. He gives Papá a homemade remedy to help with the pain and infection. We are gladly able to pay.

We nurse it as much as we can along the way, to no avail, especially without the proper rest or care. He has walked many miles with some trouble. Long distances are debilitating him quickly. I want to help, but I can't get a job because people who can use my labor don't trust that I can do it at my age. There is not much for a child of 12 to do for pay.

We walk and I hold him up as he hobbles along the trials. I search along the way and find the perfect length stick up to his shoulder. I carve it out and make a square at the top and add a piece of a shirt to make a comfortable pad for him. He can now rest his shoulder and weight on it. It is a homemade crutch, sustaining him so I don't have to carry his weight. His health is becoming more delicate and unstable at his age of 48.

Other injuries he's never complained about attained on the job are now showing signs of the damage they've caused. In an accident in another mine, a boulder wounded him when it fell on his shoulder and down to his foot. He recovered before, and we know he will do so again.

I see his face and know he's feeling the pressure of everything, and is watchful and sensitive to becoming a burden.

"I don't know if I can make it on this injured leg, mijo," he tells me one night. "I can't walk well. You may need to go on your own."

I am devastated and alarmed. I cannot imagine my world without him. I will never leave him out there to fend for himself. Just as I had not known what to expect in moving from Arizona into Mexico, without a second thought, he tethered our fears and never left us. I could not foresee myself being alone and it is not an option to leave him as if he didn't exist. We have already left my mother behind in a grave in Arizona, and Mamá Angelita in a grave in her hometown. Papá is the only person in the world that matters to me. I will not be deprived of his love, nor he of mine. We will see him through.

"There is no way I will leave you behind, Papá! I need you," I tell him when we are sitting together. "And thennnnnnn who will stay and help you?" I say hoping to make him smile. "I love you," I say in a small voice. He holds my head to his chest and this time I hug him real hard.

We need some help getting him further up to another place, so I ask him if El Bonito can carry him part of the way. Papa said El Bonito is not strong enough to carry a tall man like him as his legs would drag on the ground.

It's the first time I think of the rest of our family and wonder where they are. It has occurred to me that Papá can die out here and I won't know what to do. Where is my brother Manuel to help us? What happened to all of them, where did they go? We are so far away from where we started out at the border, so few people around, and I have no means to search for them. But we are heading back north and I expect to get him there.

We push further along, with his dream of reaching the United States now starting to occupy all my thoughts. At times it is a lonely and scary journey. The possibility crosses my mind that I wouldn't know how to get home without him. Wherever home is. If he is trying this hard, surely there has to be a real reason and a reward at the end of the road. I dare not ask him directions on returning for fear he'll think I'm giving up on him.

There are very few people on these roads, mainly because the larger towns are far apart with only a couple in between. Most people won't chance walking a long distance to a place where it might be worse. I think we are among the minority of those who risk doing this; and it's because we have to.

I know that Papá's only goal is now focused on reaching the United States. I am convinced we will do it.

We still face each day hopeful – the tomorrow we are waiting for arrives each morning -- yet I have a vague feeling of absence.

CHAPTER 6

Lessons on Love and Death
1936

We leave Minitas and a bad memory behind, and we eventually come out of the wilderness into what I hope will be easier terrain for Papá to navigate. Directionally, the way has become clearer for me.

Papá never complains but by now I can sense his feelings and I can predict his moves about almost anything before he makes them. He is rational and very logical and most days has answers to life's challenges. I see that he is very tired and disillusioned with our meager living in Mexico and how much more difficult our lives have become. He is certain that if we can only make it back to the United States, we will have a chance to improve our circumstances. He is legally able to work there again without the others because he has documentation.

He assures me that because I was born in the U.S. I should be able to get documentation somewhere at the border. And does Papá really think we'll make it back across the U.S. border? He wants for my brother and me to have an easier time making our livelihood, but so far there are no avenues opening up to any of us. I still don't even know where my brother is.

We are still going northwest toward the Sierra Madre mountain range. Papá draws maps on the ground to help me understand the geography of what he audibly shares with me. I think he is sensing my fear but I feel at one with him. I have no concept of how far it really is until I see those drawings and realize where we have already trekked. It is a huge distance away and while it's an accomplishment, I worry that we'll never get there.

His leg, his disability and inability to earn a living, along with the terrain – none of this is in our favor. It is reassuring to me that he's been that route before so we don't get lost. I am beginning to understand the depth and meaning of our trip, and although I trust Papá with my life, I am beginning to question his dream.

There are days that I dislike a lot: walking in the heat with sweat pouring down our faces, the itchy chiggers, the cold rain, walking, sleeping, more walking up and down mountains with no end in sight. A mile feels like five each day we are on the road. But I am most afraid of the incidents that we might face without Papá being able to help. He's vulnerable from every direction from the infection that won't heal. It seems to be getting worse; the infection area getting bigger, redder and more irritated, with pus beginning to ooze. Those are the things I dread, and how they will affect our lives. Our future is so uncertain but I learn to accept it as it comes. Aside from Papá's deteriorating health, not too much truly shocks me now. I just get past it.

Nearing Ciudad Obregon:

On our next stop, a man who sees Papá's condition and his inability to walk with his homemade crutch comes up to us. He asks about our trip. I think he doesn't want to embarrass Papá by asking about his leg, which looks like it's ready to burst. We have a contact where Papá has asked for lodging for us.

He looks at me and says: "If you want to earn some money, I can show you how to clean some "cebollín" (freshly picked small white onions) so you can buy something to eat."

We are destitute and it shows. Papá must be humbled, and possibly humiliated to be rendered helpless, to be in this condition with no way to provide. I look at him for approval. He nods his head and motions for me to go. I can feel he's proud of me for always being willing to carry the load.

I thank the man and go with him while Papá walks to an acquaintance's shack to rest. We are appreciative for their hospitality and happy to have the chance to do something meaningful and valuable for us. I catch on quickly and the man is patient and kind to me. Within days we have full stomachs and food to take with us. It doesn't take much for Papá and me to find something to be grateful for.

"Panza llena, corazon contento," we sing-song that line, smiling at each other after eating. We have a full tummy, happy heart, once again.

"Mijo, there will always be some kind of lack, but at least we have our daily meal," Papá tells me. Sharing food together is an unspoken celebration.

It is obvious to anyone that Papá won't survive much longer on that leg. The man who allows me to work also offers the help of a friend who can drain the leg once more before we leave. We take him up on it.

We have saved a few pesos and Papá now has enough to pay someone with a truck to take us to Hermosillo, a larger city where transportation is available.

We are into Ciudad Obregon and, although it's in the early development stages, I find it is a little more civilized place than where we have been. There are cars, people selling fruits and vegetables on the main road, with an overall busy feeling. There are small homes being built up into better ones than the shacks I've seen elsewhere.

We stay there a day while Papá visits a friend and he renews his bandage, and then move on. We have crossed many miles over much challenging landscape whose beauty and rivers inspire and cause awe in me.

We have made temporary connections with people we may never see again. Papá often tells me stories of their own survival heading north from this very area before I was born. I am an avid listener, committing most everything to memory.

On the way out of the town, we make an unexpected stop on the outskirts north of there, getting closer to our destination. There is a village named Cajéme where some young Yaqui Indian girls are out on the road practicing their cultural dances. They try to teach me the cultural meaning of the dance and how to do the steps. Their innocence is visible. Their eyes smile, and tight-lipped and closed mouths, they watch me as I try to get it. That's when we all decide that I will need lots of help in rhythm and the movement of my feet. We all laugh at my clumsiness. This is the first group of young people my age that I have fun with. It feels great to associate with them.

Growing up and maturing causes me to grasp more fully the fact that we have survived several difficult years' trek through the rugged mountains of Mexico.

I imagine that Papá's trip north had been worse at that time than it is for us now. And how difficult it must have been for him to care for me, a mere child when we started. I'm certain his life would be easier without me but he never mentions it. But then how would he have made it without my help? I am his student and I mirror him as much as possible. We are a good match.

In spite of all the walking, however, it seems that there is still so much distance to cover. We know where we want to end up, but it's taking forever and it is hard to reach. Not knowing where family ended up, we can't even claim to have something or someone waiting for us anywhere. When and where will we find some permanence?

El Bonito's Accident:
Chicural/Ciudad Obregon

Aside from the surprise meal ticket I was given in the third grade, another incident affects my outlook on life more profoundly.

We walk a few miles and end up on the Chicural Ranch. Heading north, we are nearer to the Arizona/Mexico border again but still about 400 miles south. We stay and earn a little money in a couple of towns for a while. Thankfully, although slowly, we are getting closer to Nogales – the border town we now have to reach to cross back.

At that ranch, we meet Agusto and Antonio, a man and young son team who also work there. Agusto carries a rifle at all times. We are kind of interested in why he does so, but neither he nor Antonio ever say why. It doesn't seem like much bad would go on out here in the smaller places outside of town. Everyone knows everyone else like family. Papá and he develop a friendship.

Antonio and I are both 13. We become buddies. We start hanging out near the creek, climbing trees and throwing rocks. Once I saw him dive into the river and I tried it too. I dove into a hard rocky bottom about seven inches deep and I bombed. I am lucky only my face was scraped, and no serious injury came to me from that. Antonio and I laughed hard and we became good friends for the duration of our stay. He also told me how to dive properly, but when I couldn't do it, that's how I also learned I didn't know how to swim. I decided not to try it again.

We are preparing to leave in a few days. We pack up our few belongings, mostly food, on El Bonito's back. He is rather small and can't seem to carry a lot of weight. That's why we never put Papá on his back.

Antonio decides to walk a short distance with us on our way out of town. It's such a nice gesture that many people make on saying goodbye. It makes me happy that he's doing that, but don't like leaving him behind. I'd like him to be my brother.

As we walk on a trail near the edge of a steep cliff, El Bonito suddenly seems to be spooked by something and he gets too close to the edge of the mountain, where a gorge lays below. He slips on some rocks, falling backwards on his tail right at the edge, about 15 feet and he is unable to grasp onto anything. Antonio and I pull on the rope he has around his neck to draw him back toward us, but it's useless. He is much too heavy and we're afraid he'll pull us down with him, and concerned he'll choke. Papá can't help. As if in slow motion, El Bonito keeps slipping down the mountain on his rear; all four legs are up toward us. We see him slip further down with our supplies on his back. We hear no sound for a short while, until we can't see him and everything has become quiet. Our mouths agape, it seems to take forever. We know he's finally landed at the bottom of the abyss when we hear a loud and hopelessly empty thud and one last bellow from him, from about 500 feet down.

The loud sound emanates from deep within him. The echo through the mountains magnifies it in my ears. From the top of the mountain, somehow Papá can tell that El Bonito has broken his back.

He seems to instinctively know everything. He moves over at the top of the trail to a place from where he can see El Bonito at the bottom and he waives us over to him. We follow.

"Go down there and see how he is," says Papá. I am certain Papá already knows.

Being still close to the ranch, I am grateful that Antonio is with us to help out. We go down into the canyon as fast as we can to carry out Papá's instructions, although I don't know what they are. Now I'm desperate. I don't know what to do.

When we reach the bottom, El Bonito's cries resume when I touch his back. He tries to pull his head around to his side to bite me but he is unable to.

"Take that short, thick branch with a big head on it, that old one laying close by," Papá yells down at us. "Hit him on the head several times as hard as you can!" With the echo reverberating in my ears, I'm not sure I heard him correctly so I yell back up to say it again.

"Take that stocky branch and hit him on the head with it as hard as you can. You need to put him out of his pain!" he yells again.

I did hear him correctly. Does he really want us to do that? I'm 13 years old. How can I do that? I stand by and watch el Bonito's pain, plank ready in hand. Antonio wants nothing to do with it and steps back. Always the obedient one, I do what I am told to do. Holding back tears, I hit El Bonito on the head a few times, hoping he'll stop breathing soon. It seems like everything takes forever but he finally takes a deep, deep breath. There is a rattling sound, and he stops moving. His heart is no longer jumping out of his chest. He closes his eyes and even though I'm afraid to touch him now, I do. Neither Antonio nor I feel a heartbeat.

Without a word, we gather up a few necessities from the backpack. After much struggle we are able to roll El Bonito over just enough to remove the backpack from him. And then Antonio helps me pull the heavy carcass dragging him a little at a time out of the trail-way and farther into the canyon. Vultures circle above already.

My heart hurts. I want to yell and cry. Papá knew that there was nothing more we could have done. Antonio and I walk back up the mountain taking turns carrying the sack we will take on our trip. I am a youngster with a strong sense of right and wrong. Papá frequently instructs me on how to do things he can no longer do because of his infected, damaged leg. This is harder than usual.

We reorganize and we say goodbye to Antonio and head north. I become more and more grateful to come across so many small towns where we make acquaintances and Papá can at least get some occasional attention. I am always hopeful that he will recover. Whenever and as often as we can, we drain out the pus together and bandage up his leg.

CHAPTER 7

Transportation:
1935-1939

We are ecstatic to know that once we arrive at the next mining town of La Colorada, we will be able to pay someone to take us into Hermosillo, the biggest city so far with vehicles and trains. We are very, very close.

Hermosillo

We are now only 172 miles from Nogales, the border town where our deportation from another country happened about seven years ago. I am becoming a young man.

We have trekked a total of almost 800 miles south and back up north to reach the American border again.

It is a strange feeling to go from a wilderness environment, a rural area without a population where shacks sit far apart. This city is hustling with people trying to earn their living. We are here, thankfully to take a break from walking, and we find a train to take us to Nogales.

It seems surreal that we are this close after being gone for so long. Our destination is clear now. I am getting more hopeful that we will make it.

I am elated to be on this ride again, but realize I can't play conductor and that I probably won't become one. My outlook on life has changed and the view is different for me. I've become older and wiser and I see that life is about survival. I am sure that Papá doesn't have much of a chance at surviving his serious ailment. I can see he's in extreme pain although he tries to hide it from me.

I enjoy the ride and look out the window for a long time. Neither Papá nor I say much. Along with being optimistic about returning to America, I also wonder why we can't stay here in Hermosillo. We are tired of walking. But I understand that we are getting nearer to the long-desired place Papá wants to be and belongs: the United States. He needs to return to what he considered his land, as Mamá Angelita returned to hers.

The Border! We have arrived!

Pulling up into the train stop in Nogales, my conviction to go back to Arizona suddenly intensifies as I see the Border Station about 300 feet from us. So close. We are right in front of a weak chain link fence at the invisible international dividing line once again. We have arrived!

Within a few days I realize we are back to the same dismal situation there, without a break to earn any money. I wonder how long it'll take us to get past that station. My optimism fades with a lack of money, but I cannot let Papá see my discouraged heart. Ever the optimist, he's still eager to make progress to the other side.

Nogales has grown and its people are still striving to make it. There is the hurry and wait to get nowhere. As the Great Depression has been overcome, business has improved. There are more Mexican salespeople trying to sell goods at storefronts to American tourists. The border being so close to the stores creates the majority of commerce. The same twenty-word memorized, accentuated English sentence comes from the mouths of those trying to sell on the streets and at the stores.

But there is still not much opportunity for us to make a decent living. We are not qualified to succeed in sales. I'm not a swindler trying to make deals. Papá can't manage being on his feet any more, so it's become essential that I find a stable job. Once again, I am stuck in a 14-year-old's body with the mind of a grown-up, trying to help out in some way. I have toiled in a couple of fields with and without Papá and I trust my skill. I just need a chance to prove myself. I will not give up.

It has taken three years from San Jose de Gracia where Mamá Angelita was buried, for Papá's condition to get to this point. By now his leg is not just infected, it looks dead.

But it may be possible that we will finally be able to get him some real medical attention here. It has turned from a pus-filled sac to an ugly dark greenish- purple; it is more swollen, and looking worse than ever. He has developed and is carrying a heavy weight on his body because he cannot walk.

Living here, however, is slightly better than out in the woods. Water is delivered up and down the unpaved streets by water trucks. People run out to put their buckets under the spouts along the sides of the trucks. The wet smell of dirt is agreeable and the water keeps the dust to a lesser level. People sit outside to enjoy one of life's little pleasures. In other places we had had to go find water in creeks, carry it, and boil it for everything. We still boil it, but it is more convenient to get and less time consuming.

Papá has made advance arrangements with a friend to take a message for us to stay at a woman's house for a while. I immediately go searching almost everywhere for a job. Most people don't have money to pay, so I walk up and start helping a man tear down a house, hoping for pay. At times he helps me out with a couple of pesos. I also deliver groceries or water when motioned over for help. I hang around outside a restaurant until one day the owner waves me over. Then he allows me to bus tables occasionally when business picks up.

With my father confined to a chair from his diseased leg now, those small jobs get us through a day. At a small store, sometimes the guy gives me extra vegetables because he knows I'll be hanging around again the next day. They get to recognize me and are comforted to know I don't steal, tempting as it may be at times.

Every single day when I sit out on a small wall in the neighborhood, I can see the U.S./Mexico border station right there. People walk north across that invisible line daily. They flash their green card or passport and they go right through. Just a few steps away from me and they are on the American side! I wonder why they return, and then realize they don't have the legal right to stay.

I'm beginning to wonder if Papá is right. Of all the things he's told me and I've believed, I question if we'll really make it to the other side. Why don't I cross the border on my own and then come back to get him? How will I make that happen? He says he has his green card, but I don't have documents. How can I get them? What will allow me through? If we were legitimately able to stay there seven years ago, then why didn't we stay? Family didn't even stick together. I haven't seen my brother Manuel in years. Look where we are now.

After re-hashing this in my mind, I come to the conclusion that I love my father more than anyone and anything, and I will do whatever is necessary for him to get well.

Desperate Times
El Tiro:

Being powerless about my own life and lamenting Papá's health are very difficult for me. He's been a good provider, a good protector and a great father. But I don't see a way out of our desperate situation. Something has to change dramatically for us to overcome this seemingly hopeless way of living. But hope and faith are all we have.

Unbelievable as it is, I tell Papá that I am leaving Nogales with a friend to go search elsewhere for ways to improve our situation, and that I will send him money as soon as I can.

Desperate to change our circumstances, I take off with José, who is three years older than I. My sincere desire to change our situation and outlook is over-powering. I feel confident this time it will be fruitful.

We hitch a ride out toward El Tiro, (the Target), a small mining town, 70 miles back to the south of Nogales. As we arrive, police apprehend us. I have no idea why we are being questioned and I fear being in trouble, for Papá's lessons have saturated my soul. After some interrogation, they let me go and they take José to jail. Without knowledge of his crime, I scrape up enough money to help pay his way out and he gets released. I find out he has stolen 11 grams of gold from someone. We go our own ways. I don't know what happened with that situation but he's never paid me back. And I instantly remember Papá telling me that he had sent money to the rancher from whom he had borrowed El Bonito. Don't owe anyone, he had said. He heeds his words.

"Remember to pick your friends according to their acts," I can hear Papa's words reverberating in my ears. Thankfully, he never found out about that.

Once in El Tiro, I am given a cot at a man's house where I pay minimal rent. We use an outhouse and I wash up wherever I can. It might be at the back of a business where there is running water, or a back yard or ranch nearby. Then I go and do odd jobs anywhere.

I haven't sent any money to Papá because I'm barely making it, but soon after my arrival, Papá must think I'm doing well because he shows up without notice! He comes into town and someone brings him to the place where I'm staying. I am shocked that he's made it back this far again, without purpose, and his reason for doing it is unclear to me. We are reverting from our goal to cross over.

His leg is hugely swollen and now looks dead, far beyond an old blackish color. The skin is dry and peeling, his toes sit immobile on his foot, and his leg dangles heavily from his knee like a weight. I am sure all his nerves are dead. I am distressed. That is a bad image to have to remember for the rest of my life. I want to get it fixed as soon as possible. But no one has any money to lend and I have no job.

I am distressed. I need to settle down; either stay or go, but I need stabilization.

During all that time that Papá and I were gone into the wilderness and mountains of Mexico, we had never had contact with my brother Manuel, now 19. He didn't know where we were, and I certainly didn't know where to locate him. Even in Nogales, I never saw or ran into him while we were there for a while. No connection. But as far away physically and emotionally as we are from each other now, through word of mouth we hear that he has been running a hotel in Nogales for two years. Maybe there's the opening for me, after all.

In a sudden move we are thrown into a better position. By happenstance and perfect timing, and as a jolt, Manuel shows up in El Tiro just as we are planning to leave! Our situation so bleak, he arranges for us to get back to Nogales. And everything changes.

When we leave El Tiro, it will not be a lost cause to have been there, for that is where I will meet the girl who later becomes the love of my life. The one I will ultimately marry. But it will not be without its difficulties that our relationship will evolve.

Full-time Employment:

Once we get back to Nogales, I can see that somehow Manuel has settled into a comfortable lifestyle and I don't know how he did that. I wish we had known before that he was doing well. Papá might have already gotten some help. We find a small place to live and Manuel says he thinks we might stay here permanently so Papá can truly get his leg fixed.

Manuel gets me a job at the same hotel. That's a new possibility and it may be what Papá and I need to finally make our way North.

I don't know what I'll be doing on the job, and he explains nothing to me, but I'm willing to earn our livelihood. I'm feeling grown-up and know this is the break I've been waiting for.

I show up for the night shift as he instructs me. When he and I walk in, two young girls of about my age with very rounded hips walk up to a couple of men and take them into a hallway. In the lobby I hear murmuring and slight chuckles from feminine voices when we walk by: "green eyes," "well, look at him," "big shoes, good boy."

I get a little nervous but I follow Manuel. We walk into a larger room where there are about ten ladies, young and older, situated in different places within my sight. Some are sitting at a darkly lit bar, others are seated on worn couches or big tufted chairs. There are a couple more women walking into the hallway with a man on their arm. The ladies represent all colors and shapes. I see black hair, red hair, brown hair and a couple of blondes, all with lots of make-up on. It seems the red lipstick tops it off for all of them. It stands out. Some are wearing short, tight fitting dresses with black lacing up the front that looks like they have a hard time breathing, but their waists are tiny. They have on black mesh stockings and their hair is done up. Some look attractive.

A couple of heavier ladies are by the end of the bar with their cigarettes hanging from their lips, checking me out. I've never been in a hotel where people stay, but I am sure this is not a hotel. No one seems to be sleepy but the men do look tired.

The room's secrets are hidden in the dim lights day or night, velveteen red wallpaper lines one end of the wall. Several doors lead into a hallway at the other end, going into private rooms. One of two ladies working in partnership with a man hands him a drink, each lady whispering in each ear and holding his hand to their breasts. Both ladies fake-smile at something one says that is known only to them. The man is elated and doesn't seem to notice.

Manuel and I get just beyond that area and into a different hallway. I act as if this looks like a normal job, and I ask Manuel what I'll be doing.

"These ladies entertain men and help them relax after a hard day's work," he starts out. I'm wondering where they found employment. Prior to this I haven't found a job!

"You'll be helping clean up," he continues, "picking up towels, sheets and trash from the rooms every time they become empty. You have to hustle because sometimes guests only come in for a couple of hours. Try to stay out of this area," he says, pointing to the seedy living room.

When I clean the first room, I clearly get that this hotel is a house of prostitution. Papa has told me about them, but only that they exist. Never more than that. I doubt he knows Manuel is using his immoral skills here. He would neither approve of this job nor allow me to do the same, but we need money.

I see couples going in and out of rooms, hear quiet murmurings of pleasure and sounds of excitement through the walls. This work in the heat of passion is easy compared to our physical exertion in heat of the day.

Manuel is 19 and does things that are beyond his years. The next day, I see him slipping in and out of a room with the manager of the hotel. I find out he lives there and is involved with her. I doubt Papá would see Manuel's job contributing to the making of a man or bringing him any integrity.

A few weeks later Manuel and his girlfriend ask me to watch the hotel over a weekend when they go out of town. Manuel knows I'm quick in math, and he asks me to take in and protect the money for the place. I gladly agree and see it as a fun challenge.

I have been drinking alcohol in a controlled environment so my father will never see me drunk. It's a sign of respect for a parent that a son abstain from it until someone of esteem close to the family introduces him to it. I just don't know when that will be for me.

The night when I am watching the hotel is very interesting, and it becomes a stepping-stone to my manhood in more ways than one. A couple of the ladies come up to me and start flirting. They offer me a drink but I don't take it. I'm on the clock.

The youngest one, 17, comes up and smiles and rubs my hair, softly breathes into my ear, mildly sucks my earlobe and rubs her body up against mine. She's murmuring things I am taking in loud and clear while her hands explore my body.

She never kisses me on the lips. She asks if I'd like a drink and to go into a room. I finally take the drink to ease my excitement. At my age, the drink with a soft body against mine is a most difficult proposition to ignore. I am ready to go with her, but I remember Manuel and my promise to him. I step away. I tell her I'll be done at 6 a.m. She looks disgusted when she walks away.

I keep my eye on her as much as possible that night. I resist the other ladies' continued teasing to drink just a little more, wise to the fact that they want to get me drunk so they can steal the money I have taken in. I do not want to be responsible for that.

Two more ladies step up close to my face. The bigger lady that stands at the end of the bar with the hanging cigarette from her left lip steps up to me, grossly parts her lips and blows smoke in my face. I think she's the madam. The other one steps right in front of me with her cigarette between her fingers waiving it through the air, and she tells me straight up:

"Look, sonny. Your brother doesn't care if you take a little money. He has no conscience when he does it, why can't you? We can split some of it and Patricia will never suspect. She lives in her head, too drunk to know what's going on," she says, trying to be nice.

"Okay, let me think about it," I say to her planning my next move. "I don't want Manuel to know, and I need to keep my job. I don't want any problems."

I really want Manuel to trust me and be proud of me. It's getting busier in the hotel and just as soon as the women step away to entertain clients, I make my move. I lean down under the counter and take the small shoebox with the money in it and sneak upstairs. I carry it up to a room that is seldom used but for old brooms, mops, and some old towels used as cleaning rags that don't get washed. Some are strewn on the floor. I take an old pillow from the floor and remove the stuffing. I put the box inside and put the stuffing back in around it, leaving no trace of loose filling. I then put the pillow back on the floor with the other one on top, to look messy. Nothing seems out of place.

When I return, I am tucking my shirt into my pants. It helps that the 17-year old is not at her station. I've had my eye on her almost every night. Maybe they think I was with her, and they may have looked for the money but not found it. They will definitely not find it now.

The evening has grown late and all the other ladies seem to be distracted by entertaining men. To my relief, they have forgotten about me.

By the end of that late shift, however, I haven't forgotten the 17-year-old who teased me earlier with her beauty and lust. I proposition her for my official first-time experience. She tells me which room to meet her in.

I've never been with a real woman before, and this one is curvaceous with rounded hips, young and pretty. She has dropped her puffy hair down to her buttocks. I lean her against the door in the room and I begin running my fingers through her hair, telling her that it is beautiful. I try to kiss her lips, but she avoids mine. I suddenly realize that I am gaining knowledge of her body by the lack of space between us. The blissful sounds coming from her entice me, and her wandering hands excite me more. My breathing increases. We lay on the bed and I can't believe I'm here with her. I feel like she belongs to me but I know she belongs to many others. She is not my possession. I am just another number to her.

My time with her is pleasurable beyond my expectations. We lay together a little while afterwards. I don't know if I'm supposed to thank her or what, but my father would probably say to thank a lady. After doing so, and telling her I really enjoyed myself, I give her the money and tell her I have to leave. I hate to abandon her, but I must. I get up, dress, and I kiss her quickly on the cheek. She does not kiss back. My day has just started and I need to go home and get some rest from my night occupation. I walk out into the lobby.

I don't know how the new shift ladies know about me, but they tease and wink at each other, and why wouldn't they know? They know men. I give them a full-toothed grin when I walk by, as if it's normal for me to be doing this.

When my brother and his girlfriend return the next morning, I proudly turn in the cash. What I didn't expect, however, was the way Manuel laid into me with his complaint!

He calls me into his room and stands in front of me with a belt. I am alarmed by his threat, simply when I see him holding the belt. I suddenly see myself as the young 7-year–old he sometimes spanked to try to exert his power and teach me the lessons of life, forgetting that he knows nothing about them himself. He overlooks that I have become a man of my own, walking with Papá and absorbing all his teachings and earning his respect for several years. And where was he learning?

"Hey, brother, it's nice to have fun and all, but you can't be bedding all these ladies. When you're on the job, you gotta do right," he says. "I know you don't want me to tell Papá what you're doing so clean up your act."

I wonder why he's chastising me about this. Why is it okay for him to do these things? And take money from women? He is five years older, but his actions and vices are worse than anything I've done. Age doesn't give him a right to humiliate me after I've done the job he asked me to do. And I did it with his request in mind.

It is obvious that the women used some wicked tactic to make me look bad because they didn't get their way. He seems to think my activities and involvement with prostitutes are out of control. It was only my first time!

As big brothers in Latino culture tend to "protect" their younger siblings, he had spanked me when I was young, much younger. But now, I have grown up quite a bit - physically, intellectually, morally and street-wise. As he stands before me with a belt, I think of all the times he has not been there when Papá has needed help.

I've had enough. He will not degrade me on a personal level by trying to boss me around at the peak of my youth. I work for my living. I'm not afraid of him, and I don't want to have to stand up to him in a fit of rage. I've never experienced this anger. I don't like the prospect of someone telling me what I can and can't do when they are not an example of righteousness. Papá knows righteousness, mostly.

I go against my own standards of keeping the peace and stand up to him egging him on. I am furious that he thinks he can still do that to me, and I seriously think about hurting him.

And then Papá's words come into my head: "Don't ever kill a man for the love of a woman."

Maybe this isn't the same reason for hurting someone but I feel justified. He has never been there for me, except for bringing us to Nogales. I don't have much respect for him. Even his "job" as the drunk manager's boyfriend, the ladies say, is that of a gigolo, and they see him as a selfish taker, as he's always been. He takes in the money and I am certain anything else he can.

When he threatens to tell Papá about what I am doing, I relent from excessive behaviors. I venerate Papá and his teachings so much that I will go easy, so he will not find out. I don't want to disappoint him. Respect and principles matter more to me. I walk away from Manuel.

After that, I visit other young women occasionally and usually away from the hotel. The experience is exciting, but for some reason I am connected to the first one. Sometimes I ask her to meet me away from the hotel, but she is afraid of the repercussions. I try not too visit her too often at work. I get the feeling I am not being smart, but I am young and virile and excited about my new life. I am earning money, having fun and helping Papá in the process.

Hospital Life: 1938

This year, I leave that prostitution house for my own well-being and start working as a runner and orderly at a hospital. I am far happier doing what I want - independent of Manuel's tyranny. I am responsible for cleaning up and disposing of extracted body parts and tissue from operations. In the beginning the smell is intolerable. I wrap the organs and other dead parts from the operating rooms in butcher paper and place them into a bin. I roll it to the incinerator area and there a qualified operator does the burning at a designated time every day. After a while I become accustomed to the smell of both. Not a fun job, but it is interesting and pays for our needs.

One day I walk down the small hallway to the basement where I do my job. That is also the place where dead bodies are set up on gurneys until the Medical Examiner determines cause of death. I think then they are processed for cremation or burial and the mortuary takes them.

The bodies are usually covered up, so I can't tell if they are male or female. I think it disrespectful to look under the sheet. But this day as I walk up to a gurney, I see a dead young woman lying there uncovered. She is about 30. I notice her beautiful face first. I've never seen a face like that. She has porcelain-clear features with whitish skin dabbed with powder. Her hair is dark and she looks like a Japanese doll. A fancy flower comb is still in her hairdo. As I look at the rest of her body, her skin is mesmerizing, her red lipstick and painted-on eyebrows look professionally done. Then I stare at her nude body, perfectly shaped, lying on its side. I look at her and wonder how she died. Was she a prostitute? Where is the family? How will they tell them? The curvature of her body and the beauty of her face stay with me.

Aside from seeing this beautiful woman on her death-bed, the days are customarily dealing with diseased parts. Showing up for this job is just another opportunity to help Papá get help quicker. He's been dealing with this leg for so long that I've mostly cleaned up my act and have been saving money so I can take him to the doctor.

I am getting older and I am demoralized to see that his infection has totally taken over his life. His leg has turned fully gangrenous. He goes into the hospital for two months, and I pray for his restoration. Papá goes home not really better from his leg.

I feel bad about that bill, but in the interim I am told that the Mayor of Nogales has approved payment of our debt. What a burden was lifted from my shoulders that day. And God is in the limelight in my life again.

Papá's surgery:

Not giving up yet on Papá, I talk to Dr. Francisco Cañedo, whom I met at the hospital one day. He always says hello to me when he sees me working. He has a great reputation as a surgeon. I ask for a few minutes of his time and explain our predicament.

"Bring your father in tomorrow at 9 a.m." Dr. Cañedo tells me, no questions asked. Once again, I worry abut the cost and I wonder if he will change his mind tomorrow when he finds out we have no money. As if he couldn't tell that we are indigent?

I am elated to have someone who is qualified to check him, but mostly to give him some relief. I notify Manuel so he can be with Papá, and for once he shows up. Papá looks happy to be here the next morning. I still live on hope and some faith.

"Manuel, your leg is gangrenous," he says after an examination, "and the infection has gone into the bone."

Papá says he feels no direct pain, confirming the doctor's diagnosis. The nerves are dead. "There is no medicine or procedure that will save your leg.

It is far too advanced to operate. I will need to amputate it," Dr. Cañedo tells Papá. "Once you do the recommended exercises to help it heal, I can replace it with a wooden prosthesis." Dr. Vivar will assist.

Papá immediately agrees to the surgery. He doesn't even think it over! I am in disbelief and grieving for him. I see every limitation put on him. Of course, it is already the case. As he sees it, the pain with an amputation would eventually end, but with this infection there is no end. Anything would have been better for him. My sorrow is greater now than when we lost Mamá Angelita and El Bonito. I step outside a couple of minutes and inhale deep and exhale hard, trying to relax myself. When I return, the doctor says he's ready to start. They are missing a nurse due to short notice.

"I'll need you to hold the leg up from the ankle," he tells me.

"Excuse me?" I'm certain my eyes are popping out of my head, as big and round as grapes.

I am wondering why Manuel is no longer around. He is older than I. Papá tells me he left as soon as the doctor indicated the amputation. It seems to me that the more difficult things in our lives continue to fall on me. I've never understood him. Papá knows what I'm thinking and nods at me that it will be okay. It seems we are connected in thought.

It is gut-wrenching to go through this with Papá. Maybe Dr. Cañedo was joking, but I didn't take it that way. Maybe it is because I work in the hospital - and dispose of body parts - that he thinks I know more than I do. I don't.

When I return, Drs. Cañedo and Vivar have gloves on and they ask me to put some on also. Dr.

Cañedo helps Papá to sit on a wide chair and lean forward, with the injured leg crossed over the other knee for support. He places sheets under the leg and asks me to get a clean bucket to place underneath to catch the blood and remains. Next, he rubs iodine in both directions on the leg, up past and down beneath the knee.

Papá's amputation has to be the most painful thing he will endure physically, but not more painful than the humiliation suffered at no longer being able to provide for us. The doctor tells him he will need to hold his own leg with both hands from atop the knee when he cuts. He gives him a local anesthetic shot to numb him from the waist down and, he says, he should be ready for surgery in 15 minutes. Both doctors walk out.

But time is up quickly. The doctors return. Dr. Cañedo gives him another local anesthetic. He puts a tourniquet at the top of Papá's leg and the second doctor steps in to help. Papá grabs his own leg from just above the knee as if he has done this before, without a problem. The procedure gets underway.

What if the leg comes loose when he starts cutting? The doctor presses a long sharp knife into the tissue of the leg. The cut is quick and blood and thick pus ooze out as he cuts through the skin. Dr. Cañedo reaches for the small saw on the table, and we hear the bone crunching through. More blood squirts out and drips. I don't want to look at Papá, but I do, and see him holding steady, gritting teeth. He does not appear to be shocked, but I am. Both of us now watch the knife cut through the last nerve and skin, with the leg jerking outward in that last second. More blood drips out.

It takes about eight long minutes, the longest session of my life. When it is done, one doctor immediately applies pressure on the cut and cauterizes it, and the other one sews it up with a thick thread. Dr. Cañedo covers it up with bandages all around it. He nods, letting me know he's okay. He looks relieved. I clean up some blood and am careful not to touch Papá with my gloved hands, lean over and kiss him on the forehead. We all finally breathe again.

Dr. Vivar has wrapped the dead leg quickly in a sheet and hands it to me. Dios Mio!

I put the leg on the floor next to Papá's chair and walk outside. I am ready to choke on my thoughts. Papá is such a strong man – he ever complains. My agony is bad because there's nothing I can do to ease his pain.

When I walk back in, I'm comforted to know the doctor has given Papá a second shot and gives me two pain pills for him to take home for him. It does not seem enough for pain relief, and I sure hope it lasts.

We help him onto a bed next to the chair and he is resting. He falls asleep quickly in a bandaged half-leg. Half there, half missing. It's leaking a little bit but the doctor says everything has turned out okay. He tells me how to care for it and bandage it, shakes my hand and tells me Papá will be okay.

Dr. Cañedo sends me to the pharmacy to get two anti-pain pills be given to Papá as at home. I don't have enough money, so the pharmacist allows me to buy them on credit. I tell him I work in the hospital and will return to pay as soon as I am able. I like when people trust me. I hurry back to Papá's bedside.

"And do not worry about the cost," Dr. Cañedo finishes his treatment of Papá, as he hands me a couple of clean white sheets and a new pair of crutches. I drop my jaw, I cannot believe our blessing once again. How can I ignore that God is in the midst of this? I am overly grateful and relieved, choking with emotion. I thank them both with an obvious lump in my throat and the doctors walk out.

When Papá awakens, I give him the great news and he perks up. He reaches for my forehead and kisses it. One hour later and then two later, a nurse comes in to check on him. All good, he is ready to go home. I pick up the deadened leg from the floor and I call Nico, my ambulance driver to help me get him home. We settle him comfortably in bed and put the clean sheets at his side. The neighbor lady is there to help me with him, and I ask her to stay with him for a while.

I tell Papá I have to go bury the leg. Nico takes me back to the hospital and I walk to the receptacle where it goes. I can't bear to put it in there. Nico must've seen me standing there holding the leg in hand. He comes over and lightly taps my back without a word. I tell him I want to bury the leg in the cemetery instead of burning it. I hold back tears again. Why did it have to be this way? There had to be something better for my Papá.

Nico goes off to get some documents required to bury it. He also brings another driver to fulfill the two witnesses required. They drive me to the graveyard in the ambulance. When we arrive, I tell the guys they can leave, I will handle this alone. I sign the paper showing there are two witnesses to my action and they step away.

I dig and shovel out dirt and remove it until I reach two feet down. I place the wrapped leg into the grave. The red blood on the white sheet has turned to a sticky brown. I break the homemade crutch in half and place it with the leg. I close up the pit, smooth the dirt and put a large rock over it. I walk away without looking back.

As I learn to nurse his wound, Papá begins to recover. He does his daily exercises and I help him walk to the door and back. Soon he is walking outside on his crutches. The doctor tells us he's doing well, and after some time he's ready for prosthesis. I take him in for the replacement of his leg, at no cost again, according to Dr. Cañedo. I cannot thank God enough for his grace.

It takes Papá a little while to get used to his wooden leg and at times we joke about it.

"Papá, now you will only be able to cover half the ground we walked before, and you will be twice as slow with only half a leg," I tell him. He laughs at my dumb jokes if only to encourage me. He has a great attitude and laughter seems to be our medicine.

I am proud that he's trying so hard to walk again and I know he will feel better about himself once he's able to. I spend as much time with him as I can. I don't know what the future with him will bring. That week I return to the pharmacy and pay for the shots and pills I took on credit for Papá. The pharmacist thanks me for keeping my word and returning to pay.

I only leave his side when I go to work. I listen very carefully to his every word and his poems and the songs he sings. I memorize many of those. He has had his share of love stories; and only once years earlier at the campsite had he shared his emotions with me. I sometimes wonder about a woman he must've truly loved and I silently expect that it was my mother.

One day I happen to walk into a small store in town at the same time a clerk greets Papá, entering before me. They apparently know each other from long ago.

"Manuel! Nice to see you. I'm sorry about your leg, man, what happened?" he asks Papá. After some small talk, the clerk asks him, "Are you still with that lady and the two kids from San Jose de Gracia?" The man does not know me and has not acknowledged me yet.

Papá knows perfectly well the clerk is talking about the first woman he was with at San Jose de Gracia, prior to his accident. I knew because Mamá Angelita hinted that maybe he would stay with her. I didn't know why.

My father signals my presence to the clerk with a sideways nod and introduces me. He tells him they will discuss it another time. Knowing when to take my leave, I step out of the store anyway.

I wonder how many half-siblings I have.

Unfortunately, living with women and leaving them with child seems to be a typical way for men to carry on. American men who worked in the mines in Mexico also have that reputation; love them and leave them, return to the U.S.

Although Papá is a moral man in most regards, he is not a faithful man in his relationships with women. His lack of schooling does not stop him from teaching me logical actions and right behavior, despite falling short. He never ever returned to school.

At 15 now, I certainly don't expect to either.

I am awed by his intelligence and don't understand why he has not achieved more in his life, his injury happening only three years ago. I would love to see him working inside a building not doing such hard labor.

91

The thing that carries me through life sometimes is hearing him orate his refrains and poetry. They speak to me in a way I have to think about my relationships and understand life. When he found out I had begun to drink, he let me know that he knew about it by using this refrain, saying it but once:

"Son, you can consume alcohol, but don't let alcohol consume you." Then, addressing my other vices he reminded me of a verse by a Mexican poet:

Del placer haz poco uso, si ilusión quieres tener
Que abusando del placer, no hay placer en el abuso

Modify your use of pleasure, if illusion is your aim
Because abusing of that pleasure, there is no pleasure or gain   *(translate.google.com)*

By: Antonio Plaza Llamas

Papá is the best lesson God has ever given me. I hope to raise my children to consider the same memorized readings, poems, refrains and lessons on life. As Papá calls them: Moral Maxims

CHAPTER 8

Meeting Her, Losing Her
1938

Return to El Tiro:

As time passes, my plans to stay in Nogales are suddenly thwarted when Papá tells me he feels well enough to be on his feet. He wants to return to El Tiro! The very place we recently left because there was nothing there. I am beginning to question his thinking and decisions. He's getting around all right with his amputated leg, but he's not well enough to go back to work. What does he expect to do? How can I defy him? I begin to think of going north without him. We don't have much but almost overnight, we pack and prepare to leave.

Shortly after arriving, we find a small place with a couple of cots where an elderly woman allows us to stay in the back of her home. No facilities of any kind or sharing her home; just two cots in the back. I am not a person of faith, but I feel we are getting many breaks along the way and that God has to be looking out for us.

Panning for Gold:

Papá wants to teach me to pan for gold; small nuggets is about all we will find. But that will help us for days once we sell it to the town jeweler. We take our tools with us and go to the lower parts of the mountain where it may have rained near the creek, or even if it's dry. We are looking for a hole that is at least twenty feet deep, which has already been dug by others looking for their windfall. There are layers of different rocks and minerals, in varying colors. That indicates it may retain gold and we dig about four feet squared into the side of the hole. Then we lower a strong container with ropes on each handle and whoever is in that hole fills the bucket with the silt and dirt and sends it up.

At the top, we mash the rocks and sift that through a strainer to find the nuggets of gold. We make sure not to forget to sift through the dirt left on the ground. By the time the gold is sifted, there is a small pittance to redeem, so I place it in the palm of my hand and carefully wrap it. I take it to the town jeweler after Papá gives me an estimate of the weight and get paid. I always trust Papá's judgment because he's very close to correct weight.

We believe that all the mining has been done because we seldom find gold. But on one occasion I go out to the mining area and start carving out some hard rock that looks like gold. I take that larger piece to Papá and he tells me it's gold.

I think I've hit the jackpot! He tells me to take it to the town jeweler and he gives me more pesos for those 22 grams of gold than I've ever gotten. It helps us a whole lot and I am able to get some necessary things for Papá's health.

Much later I find out that the law says that if someone mines a certain area, that person can mark it as his or her property, and can go back and mine it within the dimensions specified by law. True or not, I regret that I've never gone back. Lack of resources is a barrier to lots of things.

I come to the realization that everything is limited everywhere. I don't like that Papá returned to El Tiro, putting us further away from the international border again. When are we crossing over? Should I go on my own? Where would I leave him? Or how can I get him across also? We don't have any money and I can't help much. I'm tired of being broke and having no safe or permanent haven. As a 15-year-old with tattered clothes and shoes, I am not likely to find employment again.

Very Lucky Break:

One day a true guardian angel was watching over me. A man whom everyone seems to know in town approaches me and tells me that he is my uncle. He looks well off and I am delighted to hear that. He wants me to follow him into a small general store. I take into account Papá's past advice about listening more than I talk. I don't know the man but I follow.

"José, please give this boy two pairs of pants, two shirts and a pair of shoes," he says when we walk in, as if he owns the store. "I'll take care of it later."

I am impressed with his command. His voice has a respectable tone, firm in his request. José and he obviously know each other. Whether the townspeople fear or respect my new uncle, and whether he pays up is unknown to me, but they did

95

what he requested. Uncle or not, I see it as a blessing in dire need. I thank God.

Taking my clothes in hand, I thank them both, shake their hands profusely and walk out. I don't have a place to clean up, since the cot I stay on is only a space to sleep. I go out into the bushes and wish for a nearby creek where I can wash up. There is none. I proudly put on the new clothes anyway. I have never worn socks and am surprised both shoes and socks fit so well. I cleanse myself when I get the opportunity. I take care of my clothes for a long time, folding them when I take them off. I care for my extra set, and hide them under the cot and I alternate wearing them so they don't wear out.

Later on when I am wearing my new clothes with Papá, I tell him about my surprise run-in with an uncle and he tells me that he is a true uncle, Epifanio, his brother. He is surprised that he's in town. He was a gambler and often won in poker around local tables in Arizona. He is also the one that left the U.S. earlier than we had, and brought his own family to Mexico before we were kicked out. He also said that when they needed help the most, that uncle had dropped off carts of food and other supplies to them in Gilbert. They had not been in touch for a few years.

There is another store where the owner knows I have a reputation for hustling at whatever prospect might come my way. He gives me credit to buy a couple of small things. Since I now have two sets of decent clothes, although worn over time, I want to feel more manly so I begin smoking regularly. He also sells me cheap cigarettes and I pay him back as soon as I can. I pick up used empty boxes of more expensive cigarettes and put my cheap ones into that branded box. I position the top of the box so it sticks out of my shirt pocket. Girls will think I am better off than my actual circumstances.

In that small town, I gather enough money to go to town hall dances, even though I have two left feet and hate dancing. That's where the action is. Since I've already experienced being with women and I am getting older, I want more of the same. In moderation, of course, as Papá would say.

I have a nice blazer that my brother gave me long ago and never thought I'd wear. It is the nicest piece of clothing I have. It covers the reality underneath. By this time, my shirts are pretty worn in the back and at the elbows that I will be better off not removing the blazer. However, one night some guy eggs me on to fight over some trivial thing I can't even remember. When it is over, I leave him on the ground. The ladies seem to think that my clothes are shredded from the struggle and they make me feel like a champ. I become a little bit of a hero with them. They all know I can't dance, but the win gains me access into their world.

Noticing their attention, I take advantage of a skill I have learned with an ear for music and poetry. I have a strong desire to buy a Hohner harmonica I have often seen in the window in a Nogales drugstore. Even though I've never had lessons, I somehow know I will be able to play it. I don't know how I know. I also have no information about branding, but this harmonica is the one I want. It takes me months to save 1.75 Mexican pesos to buy it.

I revel in the pleasure of paying for the harmonica with my own money, and teaching myself to play it. It comes naturally. I take it with me wherever I go. I am getting really good at it and sometimes it attracts passers-by and young ladies. It is also great comfort during my times alone.

Meeting her:

By 1940, it is at one of those dances that I meet Micaela. She has lived in El Tiro for the last four years but I had not met her. She is a beautiful 15 year-old girl and I am two years older. Her sisters and friends are interested in me and I play the harmonica and intermittently sing Papá's songs for them. They are usually in groups and dance to the tunes in different places around town wherever I run into them. It's true gratification to be acknowledged for that. I know the lyrics to most songs and I sing most of them because I like to.

Some people compliment my musical tone and talent. One time a friend and I go to serenade his girlfriend at her window and he asks me to sing to her instead of him singing. She falls in love with him and later tells me that she didn't find out until much later that it was I who had sung. According to them, I am responsible for their four-year-old daughter. We all chuckle at my crooning influence.

As for me, I only have eyes for the sassy girl named Micaela. My heart melts when I see her. She just wants to dance, dance, dance. The odds are against me before I compete for her love.

She tries to earn a living to help the family by selling goods like lingerie, handkerchiefs, hairpins, and socks from a large basket. She carries it on her left hip while displaying wares with her right hand. She makes her way up and down the streets, even into shacks at the end of undeveloped roads. She's not afraid of people or of starting a conversation with anyone. She gives an air of confidence but I've got her number. I like that she is a strong young girl who can defend herself and a smaller brother who tags along. She is very good at sales, ready to pull something out of her basket that might attract that specific customer. She loves to handle money and is good in math. Her teacher makes her the treasurer for school functions.

Micaela also likes drama. She performs in theatrical plays in elementary school, the only education she has accomplished. She loves to sing and dance, and dress up as different characters. She is proud of her memory and playing those parts. She is very close to her friends and I'm thinking I'm going to have to take them all on a date. Will I be able to afford it?

As I observe her through the weeks, she appears to be stuck-up. But I know she is shy with boys and she isn't very socially seasoned. Her ways of getting out of things make me laugh and appeal to me.

"Why don't we go somewhere we can talk?" I ask her trying not to be aggressive in my approach.

"What do you wanna talk about?" she asks. "We can talk here."

Ever watchful and street smart with people, even though she is very sheltered, her response makes it difficult for me to make any progress. I smile to myself.

"I just want to get to know you better," I say, though I may never get the chance.

"Why do we have to go somewhere else? You know I can't go anywhere without my sisters," she replies somewhat arrogantly and walks away. I already know that, as is the custom, there will be no date unless she is accompanied by a chaperone, or two, or three. She's also playing hard to get.

Another day I am standing on the sidelines with several guys watching girls go by, making cat-calls.

"Micaelaaaaa," I call out for her as she passes by. If I call her by name, I know she'll be friendly.

I am wrong. She doesn't reply and acts like she doesn't see me. Micaela's reputation and nickname are one and the same. They call her "Micky la Machetes," or as the name implies, always a ready warrior with machete in hand that no-one dare cross. It sure makes me wonder why I'm chasing her! She fends well for herself and her younger brother, even when there is nothing to defend. She does it with a vengeance at anyone she thinks will attempt to cause any harm. But her dramatic lack of action by walking away in this instance makes us all giggle. I've played hard to get sometimes, but Micaela really piques my interest. I have to win her over.

"Micaelaaaaa, look at me," I say again with a grin, the guys chiding me and assuring me I have no chance. She flips the side of her skirt up just a little like a folkloric dancer, as if to dismiss me, turns her head and walks away again.

"She'll never come to you, you'll never get to her," my friends echo each other's words, teasing me that I am a lost cause to her. I play along with them, but I am already in love with her. I am not giving up. I know I'll marry her, so I try harder to steal her heart. I think a woman should be a challenge to entice a man and she's doing her part.

It is necessary and appropriate to call on the parents and ask if you can date their daughters, with chaperones, of course. That can be costly because if you buy her a soft drink, you have to buy one for the chaperone(s) also.

Over time, I finally persuade her to spend her time with me in public – as I know I have no chance at any private time with her. We enjoy our outings with friends, hold hands and find it difficult to steal some time alone, or an occasional kiss. Someone is always with her. Devotion to her mother and father is primary and admirable, and similar to mine.

I know her mother does not like me. But I am finally successful at forming an official and respectful relationship with her parents when I go ask if she can be my girlfriend. They want to be sure I know the rules; yes I do, and I promise to treat her with honor. So I am allowed to continue seeing Micaela. The few minutes we steal away daily are heavenly time spent together. I have been in love with her since I met her. It is a romantic encounter and point of laughter that we treasure since she gave me such a hard time.

After a few months of meeting with her, hidden kisses, watching her dance and treating her and her friends to soft drinks, I have fallen head over heals in love with her. I try to spend time with her every day. I will marry her.

Losing Her:

The next day when I go to call on Micaela at her home, after seeing her just the previous night, I am shocked at not finding her there! Just as the moon slips away with no evidence of having existed, Micaela is gone and her sisters are not talking. No one seemsto know where she is. I am appalled that she didn't tell me anything about leaving. She gave no sign when I saw her last night that there was anything wrong between us. Where did she go?

I ask so many people who know them if they will tell me where she is. I even ask people they don't know, where she went, or why she's gone. I just saw her last night! I cannot believe that no one knows or heard anything. Someone is obviously hiding something.

It is impossible that she vanished from sight without being noticed. The neighbors won't give anything up. Were they told not to say anything? Why? No indication, no explanation. I am distraught. All I know is that Micaela is gone and my heart went with her.

In my sadness I stop playing my harmonica and singing. I continue looking for her for days in our small town. I ask all her friends in private, but they say they don't know. I walk back and forth through that village wandering like a lost soul, walking long distances, asking strangers, newcomers, anyone I can. No one knows a thing. Then I think: did her mother do something to separate us?

I tell Papá about Micaela being gone and he doesn't say anything. He knows I am disheartened and almost despondent over having lost the woman I planned to make my wife someday. I am under a spell that I've never experienced before. I cannot endure an unrequited love.

Many days later, seeing my condition by the look on my face, I suppose, Papá acknowledges my broken heart. Nothing will fill the void. Regardless of what he may know, I think his own experiences with being in love gives him enough reason to help me go find her. He gives me ten pesos for the train ride and tells me to go to Nogales to search for Micaela.

CHAPTER 9

Life Changes and World War II
1941

Looking for Her:

My heart is pounding as the train pulls into the Nogales train station. Having nowhere to stay, not knowing where to start searching, I begin my pursuit for lodging. I quickly rent a small room to stay for a few days until I get a job while I begin looking for her. My priority is to go throughout the city and to find her.

I expect to find Micaela and hear from her own lips why she left. I need to know why she is no longer interested in me, and I will live with that. But I cannot live with her walking away without explanation. I can't bear the hurt I feel that she left in such secrecy. Could her family be in trouble with the law? That is actually the last thing on my mind because her family is upstanding and has a great reputation. They are un-blemished.

A few days later as I'm walking out one morning, right around the corner from where I am staying, something familiar gets my attention. I see two girls standing by a fence talking and making gestures. Just a couple hundred feet from me, I can see her movements, her silhouette, and her voice stands out.

It is her! My heartbeat increases with excitement and my voice drops into my stomach when I see that it is her!

"Micaelaaaaa!" I yell and start running toward her.

She is with a friend, and she stops talking just long enough to look around. She starts running toward me! We fall into each other's arms. I hold her small body to mine, overjoyed that I have found her.

"Fernando! I thought I would never see you again!" she says quickly, almost crying. She hugs my neck and puts her face into my shoulder. I want to hold her forever.

"Why! Why did you leave without telling me? What are you doing here? Where's your family?" It all rushes out of me in seconds.

We hug even harder, as if we've lived a lifetime together, although we've never been intimate.

"I didn't know! I promise I didn't know! They just put me in the car that night with a few clothes and said we were leaving! How could I let you know? I didn't know what to do. My mother . . ." at a loss for words, she stops talking.

"I love you," I say to her for the first time. She looks at me and I know she understands, but she is too shy to say it back to me yet.

As I hear her tell me how it happened, I relive those moments I agonized over her not being there. But now I found her and I no longer care what her mother.... oh it doesn't matter.

I am convinced she knew nothing about the move and she was as devastated as I was. But also as joyful to have reconnected. Although we never said more about it, in our hearts we knew we would reconnect at some place, at some point. These are the things that make life worthwhile, love and survival - come what may.

She tells me that since her large family is also in need, and none could find long-lasting work in El Tiro, her older sister helped her parents get out of town and they brought her with them. The sister lives in Los Angeles and sent a stagecoach ("Diligence," as the wagons are impressively called) to bring them to Nogales. They expect there should be a better chance for employment for them here, she said. She's babysitting her godmother's children to help out.

She doesn't tell me more, but I later find out that her mother Petra's intentions were to keep Micaela away from me.

I am hoping that things work out for them because now I intend to settle down here with Micaela, forever. I know I'm going to marry her.

Shortly after, I find a regular job, where my skill with numbers pays off. A friend puts in a good reference for me and my employment begins as a bartender.

The boss puts me on the midnight shift, where the tips are good. He begins to trust me and I rapidly learn to work customers at the bar. He teaches me to make very pretty and colorful specialty drinks that attract attention. He promotes me quickly to the day shift – also lots of action at that time. Even though my English is lacking, and most of the tourist industry is from the U.S., I can still communicate with them in good-natured ways. I am quick to serve and create a relaxing atmosphere for all patrons.

World War II:

On December 7, 1941, Japan launches a surprise attack on Pearl Harbor, a U.S. Naval Base, Hawaii. Thousands of military personnel are killed; many ships, aircraft, military equipment and supplies are destroyed in the attack.

President Franklin D Roosevelt characterizes it as "a day that will live in infamy" and declares war against Japan.

Meanwhile, Europe has been at war for several years against Germany, a country led by Adolf Hitler, a man that I will characterize as a genocidal maniac. His intent is to destroy the group of Jewish people as a whole. With the bombing of Pearl Harbor and the declaration of war against Japan, the United States also decides to join the allies in Europe against Hitler and officially enters WWII.

There is a lot of patriotism and heroism going on throughout the world. Entire families have an ear to their radios in homes, business and outdoors, gathering to hear news reports of war, praying for their sons, daughters and other loved ones to be safe.

The international conflict also brings on a sense of inclusion and closeness not experienced before among people of all ethnicities. Entire families mourn; others support every soldier and loved ones involved in the battle.

To serve in the war, many Mexican men are being allowed instant U.S. citizenship by crossing at the U.S./Mexico border where I finally am. There are many young women who marry and follow the men across the border. There are also women volunteering and serving as translators, communications agents and in administrative positions. That gives them an opportunity for liberation and personal growth. Some immigrate to be allowed to serve. Many of them marry men in Mexico or in the U.S. the day before they go to war. And many of those brides transition over-night to grieving widows.

There is a huge pool of married women left behind by soldiers, or widows in mourning. As bartenders, we can see that they are available to men during the war, really testing my faithfulness to Micaela. These situations create much gossip in town and a stigma for many in similar positions.

Right to Serve in World War II:

One day, as if brought on by the sudden effect of the war, watching so many locals crossing back and forth across that line of separation, I have a flashback of Tucson. That is the town through which we came from the north to Nogales. I unexpectedly strongly recall that I was born in Gilbert, Arizona, 120 miles away from where I am! The very place from which my family was deported when I was seven! I don't have any papers to prove it, but I know that lots of young Mexican men have enlisted in the service supporting America. I could enlist and end up on the other side! This could be my chance!

I now want to serve in the military for either country. Was I born in the U.S. but forced across the Mexico border illegally to make a life here? A miserable life, with my father in pain, an existence of walking almost two thousand miles trying to survive – when there could have been a better way for both of us all along.

So now I know and believe that the U.S. is my official birthplace and I have rights, but because of our past deportation, I have made Mexico my home.

"Papá!" I hurry home to tell him of my knowledge and understanding of my situation. "I just realized what you've been trying to tell me. *I am a U.S. Citizen!* I wish you had told me outright. And now I know why you say we can have a better life."

"Mijo, at the time you and I were deported, it wouldn't have mattered because those officers were not going to listen to us," he tells me matter-of-factly. "Mamá Angelita, your brother, and two uncles were living there illegally. I could not have disputed it. It would not have been right to break up our family. So we all left."

"Papá, I want to go fight in the war," I surprise him when I say it so abruptly. I now feel that I can go comfortably for either the U.S. or Mexico. "Some friends are going and I want to help out."

"Fernandohhhh," he looks up at me from his chair without moving. He is quick to exercise his influence over me, reminding me of one fact. "Mijo, if you leave, who will watch over me? Who will give me a glass of water?" Papá says it with such a tone and cultural impact, that I instantly know I can't leave him. It was like when I would ask as a young boy to go to work with him and I knew the answer.

We both had said in unison, "and who will take care of Mamá Angelita?"

It is unusual for him to make such a seemingly selfish request. But he is disabled. His having no one to care for him would bring a quicker end to his life than might be otherwise. I decide he needs me and is trying to save me from the perils of war. It doesn't take long to decide.

"You are correct, Papá, I can't go." I feel bad for not thinking of him, and needed to hear him say that so I could remember that he had no one to rely on. My brother is not around and I can't remember the last time he came to see Papá. I think it was months ago when I left my job at the hotel. Papá is my priority.

My relationship with Micaela is going very well and I try to forget about service in the war. I had a moment of patriotism, but it is not the right thing for us. I do not want to leave her either.

I begin to read a lot more and become very informed on national and international issues. I store data in my mind that I can retrieve at any time, especially historical and political events. I remember details I use in conversations at the bar.

"Mijo, you need to think about getting married," Papá tells me around that time. Maybe he's heard about my active lifestyle. "Micaela is a great choice for a wife and she is in love with you, too."

He finishes those two lines as if my decision to marry is made. He definitely knows what I think and what I need. He does not want me to be left alone when he passes away, he says. He reminds me how lonely it can be without family. I have thought of making Micaela my wife and I wanted his approval. It is great timing and good to hear it coming from him.

And so I stay put.

CHAPTER 10

Love, Marriage and Miscarriage
1943

I have turned 20 years old and Micaela is 18. She is chaste and pure of heart with beauty that satisfies my senses everywhere I see her, smell her, and think about her. She is childlike and innocent about life, with a sassy personality that attracts me more than any other woman I've met. I am a conversationalist but quieter in demeanor.

About this time, I tell Papá that I am ready to go ask for Micaela's hand in marriage. It is customary for the father of the groom to ask for the bride-to-be to come into the family through marriage. Of course, asking in our situation is nothing fancy. But Papá has a way with words and he does an impressive job of getting them to agree, explaining that he thinks we've been in love for several years. I ask Micaela to marry me in front of her parents and all her siblings. I put a ring on her finger that I had the town jeweler make for her. It is a special moment for us. I'm not sure that my future mother-in-law Petra thinks as we do, but we are set to further our relationship.

After a long and unsullied courtship, we eventually marry by civil law in May 1943. We are not yet considered "man and wife" until after the church wedding. She remains under her parents' roof.

There is an incident that happens shortly after signing our civil wedding papers. On a day when I am present in her home, Petra slaps her! I don't know why, nor do I need to. I become very upset because my father has never raised a hand to me and I've never raised a hand to anyone, except in self-defense if a man was egging me on.

I quietly tell Micaela that she needs to put a stop to it or I will not go through with the church wedding but have her elope with me. I tell Micaela no one deserves that kind of treatment. She deserves respect.

It is a very tense moment, and I'm sure Petra thought of the scandal she did not want to see her family go through. Micaela just looks at me without knowing what to do. But she knew it was my love for her that caused me to do that. Then I walk out, leaving her to settle this with her mother.

It must've been handled through some agreement from that day on because, to my knowledge, she never struck her again. Because of that situation, Micaela learned to set her boundaries and knew what to expect in our marriage. And the incident strengthened our relationship.

I always agreed with Papá, sometimes seemingly unselfishly, but it is different with Papá and me because I never feel that he abuses me or takes advantage of me. He is kind and seldom asks for anything.

In June we marry by the church – she, in her beautiful white gown. She is a petite 98 pounds and looks immaculate at the altar.

In the past, I played my harmonica and serenaded her and, of course, all her chaperone sisters stood by at her window, I wrote poems for her and always shared them with her out of love. Now I will profess my everlasting sentiments publicly to her and watch her naturally develop into a young woman, my wife, and would-be mother of our children. Our love will last forever.

As the war continues, I commit to myself that neither economy nor prior ladies will keep us apart. Nothing. The job is paying well and I have rented an apartment and bought furniture; our new home, and the beginning of our new life.

Before the wedding I ask Micaela if she will help me take care of Papá while I work because his health is deteriorating and I have no one else to do it. He is visibly going downhill fast. She quickly approves.

Papá is unable to go to our wedding due to his health. Our special day is a blissful and beautiful celebration of love, respect, honor and hope. Lots of friends show up to enjoy our nuptials. We feel very happy and privileged.

Right after our wedding Papá goes to stay with my brother for two weeks. That gives my bride and me some time to get to know each other.

I am shocked to see Papá's condition when I pick him up at my brother's house after such a short time. He has withered away. His leg does not appear to have been cared for and it has become a life-threatening situation again. He appears worn out. It has taken a serious toll on him and his long-term condition is visibly coming to an end. I am saddened to know that his time is very limited.

Micaela stays home and gives him the best care she can. She has gotten to know him better and agrees with the things I've said about him. His disposition and respect for people are admirable. She grows to love him more in a very short time, and regards him as her second father.

Her own father Jesus comes over every morning to see Micaela and drink coffee with Papá and her. I am overjoyed to know Papá has both of them, who care about him as a loved one. They have become friends and have a lot to talk about. They both like general topics, even though Micaela's father never got to first grade due to circumstances. Unfortunately, illiteracy is a known fact among people, especially during this time of War.

One night Papá calls Micaela and me into his chamber. He talks to us a little about marriage and commitment and us helping each other out. We agree with what he tells us. And then he does the sign of the cross over our faces – breathes hard and he blesses us. Micaela and I are at peace with his blessing.

The next morning Jesus comes over to visit Papá. Micaela tells him that it's unusual for Manuel not to have gotten up. Jesus wants to go wake him and tease him, as they usually lift each other up with their bantering. He talks to Papá and there's no answer. Jesus puts his hand on Manuel's chest, no heartbeat, no inhaling or exhaling. He puts his ear to his nose, no breath or sound. He has not yet changed color, nor is his body cold. But he has passed away.

Micaela looks at the man she grew close to, understood and suffered with in his pain. She weeps in a low sound and Jesus wraps his arms around his daughter. She weeps more knowing this will be her own father some day.

I am tending bar at 6:00 a.m. and a friend comes to tell me that my one and only best friend has passed away. My beloved Papá. I stop what I'm doing. I am overwhelmed with emotion and my love for this man. My father, who allowed me to tag along with him everywhere he went, who provided for me, who taught me about life and every subject I know. The man who let me learn my own lessons and live my life as I saw best. The man who protected me around every corner and warned me of upcoming obstacles solely by his refrains and poetry. He was always there with advice, caring, and all the love he had for me. He was present in my life and he gave his all for me with the best he had – always.

I expected this day to come, but not today. I realize there is never a right time. The blessing Papá gave us last night fits right in line with what must have been his pre-conceptions. I immediately ask the boss if someone can cover my shift. I'm the only one on duty this morning till 8 a.m. He sends a message out to another bartender but he never shows up, so I have to stay until my time is up. Those are definitely the longest two hours of my life. Difficult as it is, I hurry home and I find Micaela weeping, with her father talking about Papá and the gift he was to them.

114

Micaela tells me that my brother Manuel got over there as soon as he found out about 7:00 a.m. He called the ambulance to take Papá to the mortuary. I cry for my father. I bury my head into Micaela's neck and we both cry. We want to hold each other forever.

When we see him at the mortuary, he seems very at peace. He is on a gurney and will not be embalmed. He wanted to be buried promptly, as the humble man who chose not to burden anyone. Micaela's family, my brother and I, and a few of my friends attend later that day for a viewing for a couple of hours.

He had few friends. I suppose traveling for years out in nature and not staying anywhere too long created that lifestyle for him. He didn't work for the last few years due to his badly damaged leg and inability to do much. It makes sense that he didn't associate with many people. His being confined to a chair was not a life. I am grateful to have the support of my father-in-law, Jesus. That is an honor for Papá and myself.

The funeral is held that same afternoon with a priest there to bless him. We put everyone into three cars and follow the hearse to the cemetery. When the casket is lowered into the ground, I am relieved to see he's out of pain. I will miss him terribly. My heart weeps for him when my eyes are tired of doing it.

Papá was 60. He never told me precisely where or what year he was born. Basing his age on the time he died, I figured it was in 1887 somewhere near Guadalupe y Calvo, Chihuahua, MX. It is some 280 miles east of Mamá Angelita's resting place. My own mother, Petra, would have been born in 1897, ten years younger than Papá.

His death is a very difficult time for me. I relive our moments together: the paths we walked, the nights out in the wilderness facing hunger, how we savored even the bad food - feast or famine, and we gave thanks for it. I have a lot of gratitude for the things he taught me. I reflect on the way I lived, how I live now and will in the future. His moral refrains comfort me. His words flow from my lips as I recount the hours spent with him in solitude.

I vow to create a happy home for my family, and to be a good father. We await our children with hope. I only wish Papá could have met them.

Micaela's father is one of the kindest men I have ever met. He quietly supports my loss and I know he will be there if I need him as a father figure. I love him as a person. Not so with her mother Petra. She is a strict disciplinarian and tries to slap the "children" even as adults, as long as they allow it. Strange as it may seem, it is a cultural permission granted to parents that you can strike the offspring no matter their age.

But there are incidents that help bring Micaela and me closer together as we try to overcome our grief.

We are overjoyed when Micaela comes home with great news one day.

"Fernando! I'm so happy! Can you tell?" she runs into my arms after a doctor visit, pulls away and holds her tummy.

"What? NO!" I say as if I can't tell she got the news she expected. She is so young and glowing from excitement.

"Yes! Yes!" she answers excitedly. "We are going to have a baby!"

We are joyful at the news. She is so thin and petite the doctor tells her she'll have to eat a lot more, be careful and take a lot of bed rest. Micaela tends to be very active, picky in her eating, and she likes a lot of sweets. I didn't realize until a few months after dating that she's been used to hiding candy and eating it the whole time she sells her trinkets. Here it is three months after the pregnancy and she has not gained a pound. The doctor tells her what to eat and that she seriously needs to gain weight. He reminds her that she is with child.

Our joy is cut short. Within two days, it is no longer good news for us. She experiences the pain that comes shortly after doctor's orders. Someone comes to my work to let me know that she's gone to the hospital. I rush to be with my wife and hold her while she cries. She has lost the baby. We are both devastated, but I know her pain is much greater than mine.

It takes her a few months to recover physically, but she seems to be emotionally scarred by the loss. She seems depressed; her sassiness is gone. To our consternation, there is a second instance that is just as painful in the second year of matrimony. Another dreadful visit to the hospital, another tragedy with a child lost again. I presume it's due to her size and physical weakness. She eats very little food and still weighs 98 pounds.

From now on, I know she needs better nutrition and her mother brings her things that are nutritious, healthy for her and that she loves. Warm homemade beef soup and tortillas with butter, sweet bread from the bakery, sweet rice with cinnamon and milk. Not much candy, though once in a while I sneak some to her. She puts on a little weight and I think we're doing a great job of helping her to recover. I try spending more time with her, and she begins to look and act more spirited. Her sassy is returning.

Finally, on the third try and after two whole years, our first child is born in 1945. We are thrilled at the thought of being parents. Our first-born little girl is healthy and named after both of our mothers. She is a chunky, beautiful child that keeps our hearts and attention on her. I spend time with them, proud of the first trace of my lineage.

I am content during my duty as a bartender, earning money that fills our needs, and being faithful. Micaela gives her mother some money to help their family. We also buy our first car this year, a 1929 Chevy, older but in great condition. I start to learn mechanics, do all maintenance and patch-up on anything it needs.

I try to prove myself and my love to Micaela to re-establish her trust. Her sisters act like private detectives watching my every move. I try to ignore their actions but I feel as if I am living in a fishbowl. Her mother takes every opportunity to insist on filling her mind with no good.

We continue to have babies and grow our family. Birth control is not a popular, accepted or well-known concept in the Catholic religion. We are rearing several children until she finally hears about available methods to protect herself. But apparently we are too fertile, or she doesn't want to trust the method.

Aunt #1:

During that time, I am working on a hot afternoon when a companion informs me that an elderly woman and her son are looking for me. She is at a small inexpensive motel down the road. I have no idea who that might be; I considered her to be an old aunt that lived in the states when I was small and I was very fond of her. I didn't know what had happened to her or anyone else when our family was split up.

It cannot be a previous lover, this is an elderly lady, I am told. Nogales is a small enough city that I know exactly where she is. I immediately go see what is going on. It is not the aunt I think it is. But I am amazed and happy to find another woman I also considered to be a distant aunt and godmother, and her son needing help. She was close to our family. The son is finding only small chores to do for others, and they owe the motel some money for their stay and have no means of paying for it. I immediately pay the bill and call Micaela to ask if it is acceptable to bring them home for a little while. We can figure out what to do then. Of course, she agrees. So they stay with us for a couple of weeks. I locate her daughters, my cousins, and am able to help fund her trip further south to their home in Mexico. I'm left wondering about the other aunt and if she might be able to help get us to the other side.

CHAPTER 11

"Pernicious Stranger"
1953

After Papá's death, things settle down. I have a stable job with good pay, children keep arriving, and budgeting our money is easier. However, in the back of my mind I still think of the possibility of going across the state line into the U.S. I just don't know when we'll be able to do it.

As the years progress, things are going well for Micaela and me. I am at the top of my game and feeling very confident. In my bartending job I've met a lot of people. Many are taxi drivers and we hang out after I get off my shift to talk about everything. They tease me because I continue to be faithful to Micaela. Once in a while when I drink, they ask me to recite long, well-renowned poems to them, a practice in Mexico that few can perform well. I can recite poems with emotion and effect.

Several of them come to me one day and surprise me with a proposition. They say that the Taxi Drivers' Union is having serious issues and they ask me to become a taxi driver so I can help the Union. How would I help the Union, I ask them.

Despite my third-grade education, they think I may be a good spokesperson for them. I have a way with words. My vocabulary and my knowledge are extensive. They tell me they want me to be their spokesman and represent them. Some have heard me as a public orator when I occasionally join my brother in political affairs and public discourse. The taxi drivers are looking for leadership, someone to help them be better organized, request an increase in pay and other benefits.

Police like to run the union drivers off sites so they can have their own friends transport people, taking away from the drivers' business. Corruption has always existed in most countries and this is no exception.

Maybe what keeps me here in Mexico is that the drivers stroke my ego, or I want some excitement in that capacity. Regardless of the reason, I give up the bar job and become a taxi driver. I consider my decision very seriously because now I am putting on hold my dream of going across the border, where I belong.

There are immediate issues and I seem to be the most prepared to handle them, with their participation and support, of course. The authorities pose problematic questions to certain members of the union in attempts to intimidate them. I am elected to be their union representative. As a leader among the drivers they approach me for advice whether for the Union or personal need. After all those years in the wilderness, in solitude with Papá and not moving forward, the prestige in this post is intoxicating.

On a regular work day, I catch wind of my impending arrest for trying to open a new taxicab site to gain more business. We organize ahead of time for several taxi cabs to be at the Main Plaza in support of our cause. I am prepared to resist arrest because I've obtained a signed document by a judge that relieves me of having to turn myself in. It protects me from being arrested without cause. Police are simply trying to frighten me by pushing their power and making a mockery out of me.

When the police come to detain me, the taxi drivers all step out of their cars in unison and stand outside their doors, showing their numbers. It is a great organizational tactic and show of strength. I provide my document and I am not apprehended. Officers are not pleased with the outcome. We are ecstatic with a win for the Union.

Part of my knowledge comes from life's experience and being an avid listener, like I was with Papá. I overhear many people such as lawyers and other professionals talking legal issues in cabs or in bars. I retain information for later use, as necessary. I do not consider it eavesdropping as they are having public conversations.

What I lack in education, I find in simple logic and wisdom. Thanks to Papá's teachings and what I learn in life, it serves me well as the years pass.

Soon I am elected to be the State Union Representative for Sonora. As the union begins to improve, additional drivers join. I suppose my leadership is being noticed by higher ups. Our organization's growth, and our being available to do the work they want to take from us are exposing their corruptive ways.

Every entity has its problems, and the Union is no different. Things begin to heat up for me. My brother is involved in politics and rising on the local level. Because he had learned to speak English in

Gilbert, as he practices it more, it becomes an advantage for him and his ambition. At times the Union makes propositions that he opposes. This may have also been a reason for my being elected to be the Union Representative and my staying in Mexico instead of pursuing the United States dream. Our political views and philosophy of life are conflicting more each day. I am for the people and feel that his motives are skewed. I never take any bribes.

One time he tells me that I cannot go hear a certain politician speak because he is a Communist, according to him. I am very open-minded and love politics. I've already read up on the candidate and I am very interested in hearing his views. Manuel's tone makes it a command. Instead of asking me to consider his request, I tell him that he will neither determine nor influence my political perspective and curiosity.

On a general level, there is probably no more difficult challenge for me than having to disagree with my own brother publicly. I have no doubt I am better than him at public speaking, but I wonder why it is necessary to prove that. I am up against him on issues that will affect the taxi drivers, and I'll have to fight openly for our cause. The day comes and I do not do it publicly in a political realm. Instead, I discuss some issues with him privately and help him change his mind. It saves our relationship because otherwise it would have damaged both of us. I doubt he would have noticed. I still wonder if it is worth it because I know he'll be back for something.

Dealing with Accusations of Treason:

Shortly after the action I take in representing the Union, a serious dilemma arises for me personally. It is now 1953 and I am 30 years old. My family and I are being pressed by threats and I feel we are in danger of being harmed. Friends tell me of officers coming up to Micaela and staring her down, with or without our children, I won't stand for it. At times, they step up to alert the officers of their own presence.

Now I am going to pursue my rights as a U.S. citizen. I have had a Mexican passport since 1946 and have always traveled back and forth legally across the international line without a problem, as a presumed "Mexican citizen."

Someone has reported to authorities that I am a U.S. citizen, something I know but haven't seriously thought might bear consequences for me. The informant may be an envious opponent, could be my brother, or any number of people that may be threatened by the Union's or my success. It isn't a secret that I am U.S.-born, but I've never had a birth certificate.

It is strange that about that time an acquaintance approaches me to tell me he can help me obtain my original U.S. birth certificate. And I will do what I need to do.

Here I am with my young family, 23 years after I was *illegally* deported to Mexico. I have every right to be in the United States. At this point, I'm feeling the offense, insult and injury to the core for what was done to Papá and what we endured. My determination will not be diverted.

I've lived in Mexico with my father most of my life and I have made it my home. We are fortunate not to have been separated at deportation. Where would I have ended up as a 7-year-old boy without anyone, especially my beloved Papá?

I begin to feel the weight of the situation when Mexican Immigration authorities start pressing me about my civil status. I undergo interrogations that for any other citizen would have been considered harassment. I can see that they will go to any lengths to remove me from my post and let the Taxi Union disintegrate, to the authorities' benefit. Their corruption is more prevalent and obvious during this time, and they don't like having to take a smaller piece of the pie.

A Pernicious Stranger:

They determine that I am U.S. born and don't belong in Mexico, charging me with being a "pernicious stranger." I am persecuted and authorities tell me I will be prosecuted as such.

To be called a pernicious stranger sounds like I am a fraudulent, deceptive and evil person. I soon find that the dictionary aggravates my thoughts.

Pernicious is defined as: "causing insidious harm or ruin; deadly or fatal." I know I am not a criminal or any of those things. I am exactly the opposite and am simply doing the job I've been hired to do.

Since my deportation with my family, I've made my life and settled in Nogales, Sonora, MX. I feel that I am loyal to this country. I even wanted to enlist in the Mexican military. As far as I've known, I would live in Mexico the rest of my life. This is a situation that I sincerely don't know how to handle.

I immediately seek out some assistance to determine my future. As luck or God would have it, there are often people placed in my path that help me along the way. I talk with a secretary in the Mexican immigration office who is extremely knowledgeable. She gives me more help than she will ever know. I so appreciate the advantage I am given with the information she provides. It saves me from wasting a lot of time and a whole lot more due process than I could have suffered.

She tells me about *Article 30 of the Mexican Constitution*, which applies to a person of my civil status, and will address the accusation of being charged as a pernicious stranger. I quickly read and memorize what she tells me. She explains to me and to this day I remember that she said: *"any person born outside of Mexico, of Mexican heritage, who claims Mexican citizenship, is, ultimately, Mexican."*

That law or Article of the Constitution allows me to claim my Mexican citizenship so I can continue living and working here, and it saves me from being deported from Mexico.

At this time I also begin reading and memorizing other parts of the Mexican Constitution in case I should need the information as a defense.

Again, I would have been without identity, a man without a country. But it appears now that I am a man without borders, with rights in both countries.

Aunt #2:

In the following days, possibly out of desperation, I remember having a godmother in Gilbert, AZ! This is the aunt I had wondered about after the first one appeared in Nogales. I realize that nothing is really a coincidence. I suddenly see a new avenue to pursue.

126

Visiting Gilbert, AZ:

My friend Alejandro and I make a trip to Gilbert to see if I can gain some insight or help from her to move there to make our living. It has to be better than my present situation. When I ask in town about her, I am sent to a small, private grocery store where I find her. She is up on a footstool stocking some shelves up high. I call out to her from below and ask if she has a moment to talk to me. She doesn't even look down. Her reply is not friendly. She says she has no time to take care of my need, and that it will be a while. Who knows how long that will be. She never asks who I am or what I need. Maybe she is really stressed about life, or her problems are bigger than mine, but I don't get to talk to her. I turn around to leave.

Alejandro insists that I stay and wait for her to become free.

"Wait for her to come down!" he says with some enthusiasm. "Maybe this is a rich aunt and you'll never have to work again!" He's also a dreamer.

We both laugh, but already my pride at being slighted is on the line. I like hanging around with Alejandro because he's funny, but what if he's right? No, that's not how I was raised, nor is it my mode of operation to take from someone else. I have a family and will earn our living. I expected her to at least acknowledge me. I want to leave and we walk out.

We drive around and ask someone in town about a church where I was baptized. Maybe I can get some documents on my birth. I obtain the address and we go to see a priest at St. Mary's

Church, Order of Franciscan Fathers in Phoenix, AZ.

I get my baptismal papers, showing my Catholic ceremony in that church.

A certified stamp shows:

Nogales, Arizona.
U.S. CITIZEN, #T-376-10, RT. Index;
signed by Clarence Eggler, S-10.

I am hoping that document will help me in some way to get across the border permanently.

We are almost ready to leave when I ask Alejandro to go to a certain area that I remember.

We drive around a little more and, unfortunately for me, we don't find our little shack. I see the canal nearby and know I'm very close to the location I need. There are about ten very small cottages that survived suburban development. But none are ours.

We go into a building I recognize and they confirm it was the Mexican School at one time. We sit back in the car and I slouch, leaning my head onto the back seat. I close my eyes.

Suddenly, I am in our dilapidated small cottage, with the threadbare porch where the officers stood to force us to leave the country, or go back to wherever we came from. I see the running water in the canal right by our house, where I gathered it to take to Papá and the other migrant workers. There, I stood on the edge hoping not to fall in. I think of Mamá Angelita and Papá the day we had to leave in the morning dawn when the sky was still dark. And the porch where I saw the moon and the stars and everything in between through a small hole in the roof. I wish I could have seen our future.

I sit up and tell Alejandro I'm ready to go. I expected nothing from people on this trip but was hopeful. I am grateful for what I got, and I will continue with my self-encouragement.

We leave Gilbert that day somewhat disappointed that I am unable to get what I need. I don't expect I'll return.

I did not consider myself a big believer in God, but as time passes and especially this day, I am beginning to see more and more some of the breaks I am getting in life. Until now I had seen only coincidences and good luck. But God is showing up more often.

Nogales:

One day I am sitting with an acquaintance at the bar and I hear my name called out.

"Valdez!" a guy comes up behind me and lightly slaps me on the back, surprising me with his abruptly calling out my last name. My friends usually call me by last name.

I don't know this guy's name but he hounds me to play him checkers because he wants to beat me at the game. So I play. So far, he has not been able to.

"What's your situation with the Taxi Union?" he asks. "What's going on with your citizenship? And what are you still doing in Mexico?"

As far as my relationship with this guy, we only play checkers together. I am not close to him and I am not sure I consider him a friend. Why the sudden interest in me? I am unusually wary with the present situation going on around me.

"It's heating up, not sure what to do," I tell him truthfully. I admit I can use any help. Indeed, I am wondering how I'll keep my family safe. The authorities seem to be taking more of a negative interest in me and are often too close for my liking.

"Why would you want to stay here when things are probably going to get worse for you with the Union?" he prompts me.

"I have no other resources or ideas. That is the real reason," and I tell him so. But I am also beginning to awaken to the possibility that God is favoring me more frequently. I win at checkers again and, after some small talk, he says, "Give me $2 U.S. dollars and I'll get you a new and official birth certificate."

Without questions, I pull some pesos from my wallet. Trust in this guy or not, I figure I will only lose $2 U.S. dollars if he doesn't come through. Maybe he just wants to be friends.

Two weeks later, my apprehension is lifted when I get a notarized, original birth certificate in the mail! It looks official and I am elated! I can't believe my luck, or surely another guardian angel watching over me. I have not seen that guy again.

With a new channel open to me in March of that year, I am set to make my move. I can no longer stay in Mexico. Things have reached a boiling point with the Union and it does not look like it will get any better for me. I resign my post. They understand my concerns for my family and my leaving, and we part on sincere handshakes, wishing each other success.

Using my newly acquired and confirmed

identification, I cross the border to go make my way on the U.S. side. Birth certificate in hand, I proudly enter my country of origin, the UNITED STATES OF AMERICA.

CHAPTER 12

Reclaiming my U.S. Citizenship
1953

Not long after that incident, I am very confident in seeking employment because I carry my American birth certificate wherever I go. I relocate quickly to Tucson, the closest, most logical and populated city 60 miles north of the Mexico border. I stay in an elderly woman's house and she provides a daily lunch for me, included in rent. She grows grapes, tomatoes and squash, which help. Over the next year, I eat a lot of grapes for desert.

I find a job as a laborer earning $1 a day for four days. I am working on the exterior walls of the internationally known San Xavier Del Bac Mission, known as the "White Dove of the Desert" on the Papago Indian Reservation. I learn a fable about the Mission that few know. It is about a small cat and mouse that are inlayed into the top part of the

131

three-dimensional church façade. It is said that when the cat reaches the mouse, the world will come to an end.

My life is just beginning in a world new to me. My family has not yet immigrated and I'm anxious to help them cross over as soon as possible.

The following job for me is more stable and lasts a lot longer. I go out of town to Morenci, about 175 miles east of Tucson. I do not like being away from my family, even just the 60 miles away, but now I am further from them. I can't predict when I'll be able to see them. But I will do any job that will improve our situation. I don't have a vehicle, and I ride to the job with the foreman. For two nights I sleep on the cold floor of a toolshed nearby. I suppose the other men have lodging but I don't have money to pay up front, nor do I want to say that to them. Not speaking any English, I don't say much or complain. I've been used to living without much comfort, so this is not new for me. As long as I have a stable job, this will do.

The company finds out about my sleeping arrangements and they pay for my hotel for a few days till I get settled. I share a room with a couple of other guys and pay them my part until I can get set up. Travel pay for going out of town helps with my expenses so they don't have to come out of pocket going forward.

I make enough money to send to Micaela in Mexico with someone who has transportation to Nogales. I don't know anyone but associate with Spanish speakers so I can figure out what to do. I cannot be too proud in regard to being at the mercy of others, in work, in negotiating sleeping quarters, or in pay.

I finally rent and a room from an elderly woman, where I stay for an additional four months. I feel stable in having this job. I am there all week and can now give a coworker a few dollars for gas so I can hitch a ride with him on weekends to see my family. I am delighted to see my children and Micaela.

On Sunday evenings I take a bus part-way for the return trip to Morenci. And then a coworker picks me up at a certain point to go to our bunkers. I'm glad he is reliable because I need that job. It allows me to make the trip without worrying if I'll be back on Monday. Like clockwork, I am there and ready for my assignment.

I don't recall ever missing a day on the job, even though at times I drink more than I should. My memory of Papá is enough to heed his advice about not letting alcohol consume me. I am able to control it. Congregating with the other men after a long day is fun, but my priority is now a family of eight. Seeing them and being able to provide for them is more important to me.

My employment goes well and I am usually sent to additional surrounding towns like Bisbee, Sierra Vista, Globe and Miami, AZ. Sometimes I pick up the newspaper from those towns just to read in English. I can't say I understand much of it, but I begin to realize that some of the words come from the Latin language and I am able to get the gist of the articles. I begin putting sentences together from what I read. My pronunciation is off, but I listen to the guys and take it in like a sponge. Though I don't speak the language fluently or quickly, the superintendents usually favor me for special assignments or overtime. I presume it is my ease with mathematics that allows me to lead on a project, to their benefit. Or it may be their desire to see me improving my family situation. I am picking up a lot of phrases, and I communicate enough to make myself understood. Eventually, I learn enough to carry on a conversation and am upgraded to foreman.

I am making more money. I am ambitious to gain some momentum on life and I jump at the opportunity I've been given.

8 Years Later
Our Greatest Decision
1961

Time is quickly passing by in calendar months; it's been a few years now since I began working in Arizona. But days go by slowly for me because I don't get to spend any real time with Micaela and my little tribe. The longer I am away, the more I miss them and the milestones that come and go without me being a part of their growth. It is difficult for me to leave them behind every week. The kids cry when we part, and Micaela looks sad, but she knows she has to be strong and deal with the household. It's not an easy task to round up and discipline a small tribe of eight, of all ages. She does a great job without complaint because she knows we are aiming for an enhanced life. It is hard to save money but we endure the lengthy separation for our own future. Slowly, over time we are able to save more.

I didn't expect the long-distance arrangements to last this long. I was hoping to gain some permanent comfort in residing in Tucson, some experience, learn good English and settle down here. But it has been more difficult than I anticipated with a whole brood across the border.

When I return to Nogales on weekends, my friends update me as to the problems with the Taxi Union. Things are getting worse with the politicos.

It was essential for me to remove myself from that position. With my rhetoric and history, I had hoped that the Union might find a new negotiator to create solid relationships that would help them to win. I still wish them an agreement that is fair to both parties. I gave them my best over the last few years. There was nothing left for me to do.

At last, I broke those ties that fed my ego, fed my need to stay around longer – when I should have pursued Papá's direction. I question why I stayed around that long. Maybe it was my ambition to be recognized at a public level when for so long I felt invisible to others, or maybe it was the friends that made me feel needed. My priority is now my family. We will move to the land of opportunity. I am grateful that I headed north to recreate our future – just as Papá predicted.

I am now taking advantage of my birthright by holding a job that is rightfully mine. Micaela and I have touched on the subject of all of them immigrating to be with me and our making a new life in Arizona. Her family, however, is creating more chaos than good about the distance in our relationship. They are afraid she will be by herself with the children in unknown territory when I continue to work far away. I know she has a hard time defying her mother, as I did with my father out of cultural respect, but her mother is interfering in our marriage. She does not want us to leave even though I've been a good provider, father and husband.

We seriously discuss the benefits of immigrating our family. I have often wished I could bring them over for a period of time, but their schooling and change of living would be disrupted. It is not worth a temporary arrangement at this time.

We decide to make the move. We begin making plans to go through the process for all our eight children.

I am now making about $480 U.S. dollars per month. Difficult as it becomes from every angle, familial, social, economic and domestic, under disciplined budgeting, it takes us about a year to save $250 U.S. dollars. Micaela goes several times to the U.S. Immigration and Naturalization Service Office at the Nogales border, to ensure we have all the correct information we need for each of them. We begin processing the first three U.S. resident green cards there. We are required to follow instructions and make special trips to Hermosillo, the central Immigration office in Mexico. The resident cards will be delivered when they are all ready. We are getting very hopeful.

After processing the first few applications for citizenship, I still have to obtain a $500 loan to help us make it happen for the rest of them. That money comes from a finance company and I know exactly how long it will take me to pay off that amount at those abusive interest rates. I do not yet have a working relationship with any banks so we do what we have to do.

Immigrating My Family – Crossing Over:

It is 1961 and we are ready. We have been married 18 years; have survived a long-term physically separated relationship since I came here. It's been a long eight years, and a long time coming but well worth the trials we endured. Our eldest daughter turned 16 and decided to stay behind with her new husband. I will immigrate both at a later time. In anticipation of my family's arrival here, I have rented a two-bedroom house. We will make do with what we have.

We officially go through the lengthy process, pay all the necessary fees, and finally get approval to come across permanently.

All of them swiftly and proudly cross the border to join me with heads held high and officially issued permanent resident green cards. I later immigrate the eldest and her husband, who had stayed behind, to ease Micaela's worries about her being so young and far away. Two additional children are born after this, with one of them born in Arizona. Ten kids are more than enough.

A baker's dozen would not have made us happier, as people joked. We are content and proud to raise them through love, joy and tears in the states. I am also glad that Micaela finally found a birth control method that works for both of us.

I would never accept or endanger my children to make a run for it illegally across the border. I was brought up to earn my way through anything I want to accomplish. I'm not sure if there's a hardship that could have prompted me to cross illegally. But thankfully, my family is now secure in a land where we can thrive.

CHAPTER 13

Life is Sweeter on this Side
2018

Gilbert Historical Museum, Gilbert, AZ:

I hear a car engine start up outside. It purrs quietly. I know the swift sound of a1927 Model A Ford. It's the kind of car I would buy if I could afford it. All I ever see are covered wagons passing by on our rural road in Gilbert, where they occasionally pick up Papá on his way to work. I've never been outside of here.

Alejandro is sitting at the wheel of his car looking at me, waiting for me to tell him where we are going.

I have to go find what I remember to be the Mexican School I attended in first grade. That is the small house where only Hispanic kids are taught. I am one of them but I'm not in the photo albums. Our skin and hair color and the fact that we don't speak English segregate us.

There is another small building next door only for Negro children. They speak English, but need to be placed with their own, we are told.

We go inside the building and they confirm that it used to be the school. I am able to get my attendance records proving I only showed up 16 days that year due to hardship and lack of transportation. I was there.

I hear my teacher's voice calling me again softly and then fade away. But it's Papá's voice calling that gets my attention.

"Fernandohhhh. . . Fernandohhh... it's his sing-song way of calling me.

"Papáhhhh.... Papáhhh .... I'm right here."

His memory brings me back and I'm sitting at the small desk with the large photo album in hands.

"It is beautiful here," says Micaela, jarring me back into the real world in the Museum and other people walking into the classroom. "Did I go to school here too?" she asks.

I look around the room and the innocent face and voice of my life-time friend and wife, Micaela, reminds me of the love I have for her. I'm glad to be here.

She and my daughter hug me with a tenderness and strength I only occasionally experienced in my life from Papá. My daughter's tears flow freely and I hug them both back hard, one in each arm, validating that I did exist almost a century ago, right here.

I dab between my eyes gently with my thumb and index finger. Micaela hands me a tiny hanky she carries in a purse that is about thirty years old and near empty. That and a small lotion are all she carries in there. She can't put anything of importance in there for our fear she'll misplace them.

The Mexican School was beautiful. And though it's the first time I see the Gilbert Museum, I find it beautiful also. It has been the keeper of Papá's foresight, and my dreams and hopes.

"Why are you crying? Did I go to school here with you?" Micaela asks looking from one of us to the other.

"No, Micaela," I tell her in my kindest voice. "We met in Mexico where you danced a lot until I finally caught you. Remember?" and she nods with joy. "And then I married you. But I went to school here when I was little. Remember I told you about it all those years? This is it."

I look at her with a eyes of understanding known only by those who recognize her condition with dementia. At this time it is our daughter and I. Then through a tiny glimpse of reality, Micaela's eyes shine; she smiles and opens her mouth empathetically in an aaahhhh circle. She raises her eyebrows and nods as she realizes that I escaped briefly into a part of my mind I hadn't gone before. I was there for an eternity.

"Fernando, *this* is where you went to school! Now I remember!" she says, not knowing that I just experienced a moment between pain and pleasure with our history behind us and what is left of our future waiting. Of course, she can't remember. She has never been here before today. My heart feels full.

Daughter and mother smile at each other again, confirming the sense of joy they sought to finally see me having found my peace.

This trip of a lifetime could have been made at any time, but here we are in the final phase of our lives discovering our truth, Micaela and I. Better than to never have known at all.

I am where I belong. I have been here before – Gilbert, Arizona, in 1930 – when I was 7 years old and I went to school for a few days. No one can deny me that. This is where Mamá Angelita fed us and watched over Papá and me when he and my uncles worked hard in the migrant fields, very close by.

This is the place where I was born. The place we left because we were "invited" to leave by those in authority, exercising corrupt power. They had no right to impose that on us without our consent, or without confirming that Papá and I belonged here.

And because of their having done so, without caring and in haste, we experienced life through hunger, sadness, joy, love, respect and forced humility. And Papá's painful journey and death.

The U.S. is largely responsible for the humiliation he suffered; the most unbearable for him not being able to provide for ourselves. Papá knew himself. He didn't reach his dream but his vision, like a guiding star, was enough for us to follow.

I lost my identity at the beginning of the journey, but I regained my soul. I found the courage to stand for what is right. I earned the substance of having come to know myself.

Without fully recognizing it, Micaela and I pursued Papá's dream until it became ours. It is the wish to create a family with decent children; the knowing of the value of life through his maxims of morals, and our keeping a family together to the best of our ability. It is the pride of buying a home, earning our own living and providing for our own needs without relying on someone else. And the accomplishment of crafting our own future.

We are in the coveted UNITED STATES. The land where Papá strived so hard to get back to

141

because he knew there was an opportunity awaiting us. That is the something that I doubted when I should have had faith in Papá. I am at the place I can finally call my homeland, and where our children will lay us to rest without carrying us via foot almost 1,600 miles on dirt roads, through steep mountains and storms, to get here.

CHAPTER 14

My Freedom and U. S. Redemption
Tucson, AZ
2019

Micaela and I have been married for 76 years. We sit outside on our rocker loveseat at least once a week, and we are content and at peace. As an informed man, I fought for, and won back, my U.S. birthright and American citizenship.

I labored long and hard for 32 years here in Arizona, (and about 10 years in Mexico). I did not become a conductor on a train. But if schooling had been made available to me, I could have.

Despite the hardship of being deported, not knowing where I was or where I belonged, and not speaking English, I began to know myself. I survived the trek with my father through the Sierra Madre Mountain Range, until I became a young man. Those days when Papá almost perished along the way, enduring the sickly, hungry, lonely and humiliating times, it was love and care for each other that brought us through.

The financial and emotional battle to legally immigrate nine children and a wife, with the tenth being born here, drained us of human fortitude and funds, but it also carried much joy. I am grateful for good fortune. We are thankful to have been able to help those who needed it when we could give it.

Clinging to my third-grade education and the love of learning, observant and leaning on my father's more advanced teachings, I walked through a country with no real confidence of making it back to Arizona.

My ten children have always had shelter and food. We experienced a lot of pain as a family, but there was always love and laughter in our home. One son survived two kidney transplants, three survived the military, all graduated from high school, and four have passed on. Some went on to college at their expense. All had children and only one did not marry. We also have great-grandchildren and our legacy will live on in this country.

I have been married to the same woman because we took our commitment to each other seriously, till death do us part. We always kept in mind what Papá told us about helping each other through life, and as a couple. We still hold hands when we sit under our favorite tree. We think of the luxury of having our safe haven, being debt-free and knowing that our children are all doing their best. The remaining six range in ages 55 to 74 years.

Without knowing or intent, the United States has redeemed itself in making up for my struggle and pain. I have received my retirement pay since 1984. It hasn't been given to me, I earned it and my country owes it to me.

For many years on the 3rd of the month, we waved at the mailman with the U.S.P.S. patch on his uniform sleeve. He waved back, honked once and grinned as he dropped off our Social Security checks in the mailbox. With technology, we no longer have to go to the bank.

Most people pass away shortly after going into retirement. We are still here. We have full medical care and we've now both been collecting Social Security for 34 years. That is more than $300,000 for taking a rest till the end of our lives. I'd say God has been blessing us. I've been compensated and it all happened naturally.

And now Youn'tand?

The End

This poem was written by Fernando for Micaela, part of it when they got married in 1943. It has been translated to English for this book. Although it does not rhyme in English, it does in Spanish, and the truth beneath it pierces our hearts with enduring love. Music was composed and performed to it in 2016, their 73rd anniversary.

"Our Commitment"

By Fernando Peréa Valdez
to Micaela Valenzuela Valdez
Published April 2016
Translated from Spanish

Since 1940
of the last century
Of a beautiful woman
I am still in love.

We reached an agreement
With respect for our elders
And with a kiss and a hug
in abstinence we waited.

In the year of '43
we were married through the church
we vowed always to love each other
And we've never separated

One time before an altar
I promised always to love you
and to live, woman, to adore you
I will tear my heart out if I don't love you,
and if I love you it shall be till death

God granted us ten children
and then He took away two
we could never complain
It was His will to do

Our mission was to have ten
and none was ever too many
Here we are in Tucson
I've turned 93 and you'll be 91

One time before an altar
I promised always to love you
And to live, woman, to adore you
I will tear my heart out if I don't love you,
and if I love you
It shall be till the death

*Video composed and produced by P. E. Robinson,
grandson, 2016*

https://www.youtube.com/watch?v=slKM1z47KQg&feature=youtu.be

Original Spanish Version of Poem
Composed to music June 2016

"Nuestro Compromiso"
Por Fernando Peréa Valdez
Para Micaela Valenzuela Valdez

Desde mil novecientos cuarenta (1940)
de nuestro siglo pasado
de una mujer hermosa
aun estoy enamorado

Hicimos un compromiso
y a los nuestros respetamos
con un beso y un abrazo
con abstinencia esperamos

Año del cuarenta y tres ('43)
por la iglesia nos casamos
amarnos siempre juramos
y nunca nos separamos

Una vez ante un altar juré quererte
y vivir mujer para adorarte
me arranco el Corazón si no he de amarte
y si he de amarte, ha de ser hasta la muerte

Dios nos mando diez hijos
y luego se llevo dos
y no pudimos quejarnos
fue la voluntad de Dios

Nuestra mision fueron diez
y no nos sobro ninguno
aqui estamos en Tucson
yo cumpli 93 y tu 91

Una vez ante un altar juré quererte
y vivir mujer para adorarte
me arranco el Corazón si no he de amarte
y si he de amarte, ha de ser hasta la muerte

A mi esposa, Micaela,
Con todo amor
Fernando Valdez Perea
© 2016

*Video composed and produced by P. E. Robinson,
grandson, 2016*

https://www.youtube.com/watch?v=slKM1z47KQg&feature
=youtu.be

Mr. and Mrs. Fernando Valdez, June 9, 1943

Both articles and photo below regarding the Mexican School were reproduced and used with permission from: Gilbert Heritage Museum, AZ. "From Cowboys and Sodbusters to a Mega-Residential Community," Dale C. Hallock, 2007

Gilbert Mexican School

"From the 1920s until 1951, Gilbert had a segregated school for Mexican children in grammar school. Below is a photo of the building they attended. The building is now used for accounting offices for the entire Gilbert School District.

In the 1920's, this home in Gilbert was used to teach the few black students who lived in Gilbert. The house was near the water tower but has been torn down.

In 1940, a small two-room building was built to the west of the south wing of the elementary school, providing two first-grade rooms. Mrs. Tissaw taught in the larger east-side room, and Miss Applebee taught my class on the west end in 1941.

Even though the Gilbert Elementary School continued to be used until the 1970s, new brick cottages were built for classrooms to the west and south of the old school building. These units were built in 1954 and have been used continually as they are today in 2007."

The Mexican School in Gilbert, Arizona until 1951,
courtesy of the "Cowboys and Sodbusters to a Mega-
Residential Community" book by Dale C. Hallock in
the Gilbert Heritage Museum.

Fernando attended school here at age 7 for only 16
days when was deported in 1930.

He returned various times to what is now the
Gilbert Heritage Museum to find his place and his
home.

This classroom sits in the Gilbert Heritage Museum and is a mock setting of an original one where Fernando attended school in 1930.

"Educating Children of Mexican Heritage"

"In 1927, the Gilbert School Board decided to separate children of Mexican descent from Anglo children.

This type of segregation was common in Arizona at this time. The Gilbert School district constructed a four-room building on the south side of the Gilbert High School; it was commonly called the Mexican School. Today, it serves as the business office for the Gilbert Public School District.

Often, Mexican American children began school speaking only Spanish. At school, they were only allowed to speak English, even on the playground. Many students spent two to three years in first grade learning English and acquiring the necessary skills for this grade.

There were dedicated teachers at the Mexican School but no playground facilities, no swings no balls or shade trees – "no nothing" – said Anna Marie Rosales Hernandez. The students could not use the nearby playground that was available to Anglo students. . .

Supposedly Mexican American children attended this school because they could not speak English, but some could speak English when they began school. In 1947, a group of parents and former students approached the school and asked that those speaking English be able to move into higher grades. The board determined that a language readiness test could be used for student placement. Then, in 1949 the board decided to end the separation of students and the school closed in 1951."

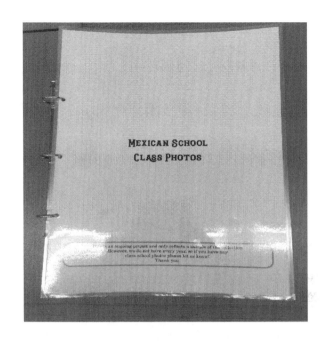

The Mexican School Class photo

Fernando Valdez' U.S. birth certificate was issued
Dec. 1952 after an acquaintance asked him for $2
U.S. dollars during their conversation, but never
told him what the money was for. Fernando gave
him the money and two weeks later received the
certificate, which he had never seen and had lived
without for all those years. It was the core reason
why he couldn't return to the U.S. He proudly
carried it in his wallet for years, tattered and torn.
He gives thanks to that man, whose name he
regrets he never got. (Fernando has a new
certificate of birth).

Fernando Valdez, age 94, where he returned to the Gilbert Heritage Museum in Arizona and where he went to school in 1930 before it was refurbished.

Fernando and Micaela Valdez at home, June 2018
At ages 95 and 93.

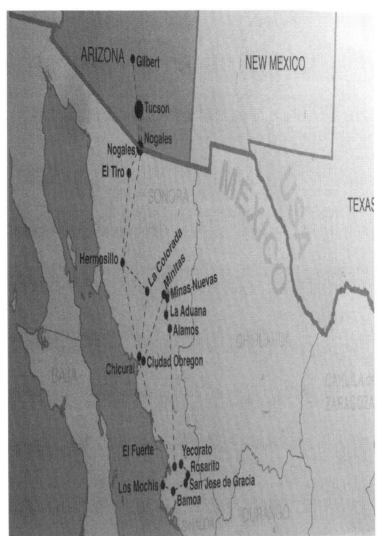

P.E. Robinson

Southbound train: Hermosillo, Son. to Bamoa, Sin.
Northbound train: Hermosillo, Son. to Nogales, Son.
Map is not to scale. Towns and cities were inserted
in approximate areas as they were visited, depicting
their trek via foot and some railways.

Very Special Thanks

I thank God first. He has provided for all our needs. I start each day with few regrets. Our parents' lives have become more important since we've had to care for them after our father survived a coma for 11 days and mother survived the trauma through her dementia in 2017.

We thank our parents, Fernando and Micaela Valdez, for sharing the hardship of their journeys, individually and together. Thank you for allowing all ten of us children to experience the *legal* process of Immigration and a better life in the United States of America. We are all U.S. citizens. It is by their love and example that we learned to be self-sufficient, productive, civic-minded citizens (three served in the military: Army, Marines and Air Force, with honorable discharge).

Thanks to our sister (Bea) Beatriz Valdez Mendez for their constant care, (24/7) and for spending many more hours than anyone else with them. She listened to the same stories and committed them to memory bringing precise detail to this book. Thank you for their continued care.

Thanks to our brother Miguel Valdez for his medical expertise, his time and interest in helping both recover when doctors gave up on our father. Thank you for tracing our lineage and family roots, and for supplying official documents.

The three of us spent six weeks nursing our father back from the brink of death. Mother, despite her dementia, helped through companionship, physical touch, and memories regained together.

Thanks to my son P. E. Robinson, who so lovingly and generously shared his knowledge in writing a novel, time and talent in editing, and designing a cover that tells the story accurately. I could not have done it without you, son. Love and thanks to your beautiful family for always being there and for their patience!

Thanks to my daughter Michelle R. Aguilar, always there to support us in everything, or a little sanity in life when we all go crazy at the same time! Thanks to your beautiful family for their patience as we all mature.

Thanks to Dr. Francisco E. Balderrama, Dean, College of Natural and Social Sciences, California State University, L.A. for helpful history and information provided. Author : *Decade of Betrayal, Mexican Repatriation in the 1930s,* and co-author Rodriguez, Raymond (Emeritus); 1996 (2nd ed. 2006) Albuquerque, NM, University of New Mexico Press.

Finally, a thank you to all who helped along the way and gave me the love and space to do this.

About the author:

Rosa Valdez-Robinson is a former reporter and freelance writer for various periodicals. She was also a junior community organizer for civil rights.

In 2008 she traveled through the Copper Canyon via train to return to her father's memories and experience to be able to one day tell his story. Publication: San Antonio Express-News, "Journey through a father's past," January 13, 2008.

She is divorced. She has two children and five grand-children, with whom she loves spending time.

Rosa lives in Colorado, where she has found her peace in the mountains. This is her first book.

Rosa Valdez -Robinson